THROUGH MYTH WE CALL ILLUSION

To Marianna
I wish You Joy, Peace,
Happiness and Love as
You walk your Path
into Enlightenment.
with Love
Orda Golden Eagle Woman

THROUGH THIS MYTH WE CALL ILLUSION

Unraveling the Mysteries of Life

Arda Golden Eagle Woman

Library of Congress Number:		2004093264
ISBN:	Hardcover	1-4134-5661-8
	Softcover	1-4134-5660-X

This book was printed in the United States of America.

To order additional copies of this book, contact:
Xlibris Corporation
1-888-795-4274
www.Xlibris.com
Orders@Xlibris.com
24427

CONTENTS

DEDICATION

I am eternally grateful to the Masters and Angels, whose loving guidance and uplifting messages landed me safely above Illusion's negative clutches. Without them, I never would have made it

I especially thank Lord Jesus, Mother Mary, Archangel Michael, The Council of Twelve, Spirit of Enlightenment, ShaLanda and MeAmba.

My thanks also to those who assisted me in co-creating the many experiences for my evolvement, in this and other lifetimes, I trust I touched their lives as deeply as they did mine.

Thanks for the ride. It's been quite a trip—to say the least.

This story is a reflection of life, weaving a picture of how past lifetimes affect our present one. Let yourself flow with the story as it evolves, and allow the answers to surface. For life is a Cosmic Joke until we find the missing pieces to the puzzle. When we do, then the picture becomes whole, and all is made clear.

Life's Cosmic Joke

Walking through this Illusion we call Life
Dancing in its madness
Loving Life in all its forms
Searching for the Answers

Life is One Big Cosmic Joke
No sense, no rhyme, no reason
A hodge podge, roller coaster ride
A jumbled picture puzzle

Take Life's bag, shake it well
Draw from it the pieces
Walk through its maze until you find
The path that you have chosen

Allow with Love the picture
To unfold, to come together
See, Life really does make sense
Once the Joke is mastered

INTRODUCTION

We are all chameleons, ever changing, ever stretching, ever reaching toward the light and the truth of who we are. We are the dramatization of our creations. The more we dramatize, the more solid the illusion and, because we judge it, the more stuck we become within it. What a wonderful, crazy and exciting game we have chosen for ourselves here on beautiful planet Earth.

Where did it cease to be fun and become the deadly serious game of survival? I have spent many lifetimes not only creating and dramatizing new and different illusions, but getting caught up in them as well. Being an old soul, I became quite adept at creating and dramatizing new and different ones. If practice makes perfect, then I should really have that one down pat.

What a long, strange journey this has been, only to end up back where I started, in The Golden Sea of God's Unconditional Love. And what an awakening it has been, for me to find that I have come full circle.

How many lifetimes did I have to go through until finally "seeing the Light?" Well, more than I would like to admit. Was it all worth it? Earlier you probably would have heard me say, "nothing could possibly be worth this." However, now I am very happy to say YES! Believe me, the results have been highly rewarding, to say the least.

I thank my angels, or whoever was guiding, pushing, shoving, and even sometimes kicking me in the rear, but always with love and encouragement, so that I would never give up. These different and sometimes difficult experiences have given me a knowingness which no gold or money could ever buy.

Besides, had I given up, there would still be many fragmented parts of me out there waiting to be recognized and loved. Thus I would never have known this wonderful feeling of wholeness—of knowing who I really am, being in the now and, most important of all, loving myself unconditionally. Believe me, this in itself is worth the price of admission any day. I couldn't have given up anyway, for that wasn't part of the contract.

One thing, among many, that I received from all this is the Awareness, Love and Light, which is true power. The way I look at it is, that before I could be of any real service to the Light, I had to expand my awareness, my love, my compassion and also my knowledge of how to best deal with less than positive energies on planet Earth. She is a wonderful training ground to experience, as I learned how to handle the negative energies, turning them to light. Having experienced, I now am ready to fulfill my mission.

We all agree on one level or another to everything that we have ever experienced, or we wouldn't be experiencing it. The bottom line is that I have, through these many lifetimes, experienced and am now remembering. I know what it feels like to fear, to be ill, to die, to be born, to judge. Mental and physical pain, as well as loneliness has always been close companions for most of us—part of our training in learning to handle negative energies.

Through these many experiences I have, with the help of my many Angels, learned to let go of fear and to love unconditionally. In doing so, I can now assist others by bringing them to the understanding of what they are creating for themselves through cause and effect. When you create within negative vibrations, you then receive negative results. But create in love and joy, and the world is yours.

Come walk with me as we journey through the labyrinth of this and other lifetimes. Perhaps you will see glimpses of yourself along the way, which will open up memories of long ago, when you, too, were in that Golden Sea of Love. You may even begin to recall your own commitment to assist in bringing The Divine Plan into fulfillment.

If I can unlock some of these doors so that you may enter into your own almost forgotten memories of who you are, beholding the treasures awaiting you, then I will be fulfilling my own commitment, which I made so long ago.

The time has come for each of us to realize the truth of who we are. God's Golden Sea of Unconditional Love and Light awaits you. Awaken to Its beautiful vibration, which is your own true essence. Once you have returned to that essence, the longing, the loneliness, the searching will be ended. You will have come home.

ENJOY YOUR JOURNEY

THE BIG BANG—THE DANCE BEGINS

At first there was only a deep penetrating silence, and a feeling of movement—a vast ocean of darkness singing a soothing lullaby without sound, music or words. There was an awareness of being everything and yet being nothing, of one heart beating in perfect rhythm with no separation, only oneness.

Then began a movement deep within—a wave of energy coming from the very bowels of that vast stillness, sending rippling waves of energy throughout the void. The waves of energy became stronger, more powerful, and with an awesome explosion of sound, light and color that vast stillness was shattered as Mother God gave birth to Her many Spirit Children.

And so the Dance of Life began. Where once there was only one energy, one thought, one Beingness, we became many, separating, dividing again and again, becoming individualized, each vibrating in its own Signature Vibration.

Gradually I became conscious of my own vibration of separateness. I felt less than whole, and yet there was a quickening within my own

17

individual knowingness, stirring deep within. I was aware of feeling alive, of developing, growing into something I was not, but was yet to be. It was exciting, awesome, and at the same time frightening and confusing.

I became aware that I was being challenged, given a direct order— "Become! Create! Explore!" There was a feeling of being separated from those to whom I had, for so long, been attached. I felt lost— abandoned—not quite whole.

Then, with a mighty thrust of energy, we were sent on our separate ways to expand, experience, grow, create in whatever way we so chose.

And so the Oneness was no more as life in its various forms and universes began its transformation. The Oneness of The All That Is was now being reflected in various and wondrous forms, in every conceivable and inconceivable way—evolving, creating, then destroying itself only to re-create again in order to expand, to become more of who it was to be. Thus The Great I AM not only was ONE, but also became vast and varied separate Points of Light.

As individual vibrations came together once again—remaining separate in our own uniqueness, yet working as one—began the creation of worlds, galaxies. As life materialized, the formless became form and matter, ever expanding, ever evolving, destroying and then recreating itself again into new shapes and forms.

And now we are awakening to the truth of who we are—each sharing our own part of The Living Library, expanding our awareness and knowledge. The totality of the Divine Plan is being revealed, drawing us closer, back to the Oneness within the Love of THE GREAT I AM.

Yes, I remember the separation. Do you?

When
you have finished
exploring
the negative shadowy side
of self

You will be free

WHO AM I

Who am I? I look in the mirror and I see
A stranger staring at me.
Then I say, "I don't know you."
And the stranger replies, "I am you."
But if this is true, then
Who am I?

How many times have we looked in the mirror and felt that the reflection we were seeing was someone else's, not ours. Someone who seemed vaguely familiar, yet somehow unreal, not at all like what we felt we should be seeing? This then leads to asking ourselves, "Who am I, anyway?"—leaving us feeling somewhat like a stranger in a strange land.

Perhaps we even get a glimpse of being in another time, another place, but our so-called "common sense" tells us that is impossible—but is it? This is when we get into questioning, "Have I really lived before? And, if so, then am I who I think I am, or am I someone else?"

Every time we are born, every time we die, it is always a new beginning, a new chapter in our many lifetimes. So if you have asked yourself those questions, believe me, you are not alone. The veil is becoming very thin, and some of us are beginning to see that there is much more to life than what we have been led to believe.

There has been a big opening within my memory, enabling me to remember other times, other scenarios. For instance, this lifetime, when I was very young, I remembered my birth, of being held upside down by the doctor, and looking at his brown shoes.

Those brown shoes have flashed across my memory many times. In fact, for a very long time I had a deep aversion to the color brown. This must have been a carry-over from that not-so-gentle whack he gave me across my little behind. I remember letting out a howl of protest at such a rude welcoming.

Believe me, we all carry memories of past experiences, especially the traumatic ones, which can equate into some pretty weird rationale. This can distort our perception of what we are currently experiencing. So until we recognize the judgment, which created that memory and remove it, we continue allowing that which was in the past to affect our actions and reactions in our lives today.

However, upon being placed in my mother's loving arms, safe and warm, my world made sense, and I forgot all about that incident until much later. Once remembering that incident, I then became aware that I love the color brown. It was only my judgment of that past scenario, which had distorted my perception.

That feeling of being in a safe world was rather fleeting. After all, I had come to planet Earth to experience and learn, and so my education began at a very young age.

I will never forget that day. I can still see myself—a little girl, around four years old—out in the pasture, near my home, happily picking wild flowers. The smell of green grass, and the warmth of the sun drifts into my awareness as a meadowlark sings his joyful song. Everything is beautiful and my world feels so right.

Then a door in my memory clicks open, suddenly I am in another lifetime. I know who I am, and also those who shared a part in that dramatic yet very necessary play. In fact, it was a lifetime that has left

ARDA GOLDEN EAGLE WOMAN

a very big imprint upon this planet, and still does to this day. And, strangely enough, I knew that which I was seeing was as real as my current life.

There was a wondrous, joyful feeling at this tremendous revelation. This, however, was to be short-lived. Immediately thereafter I was surrounded by a warm, golden light. Then a voice, powerful, yet somehow gentle and loving said, *"YOU ARE NOT TO TELL ANYONE ABOUT THIS!"*

There was no fear. I felt surrounded in a golden glow of love. Although I did not understand why, I never said a word about that incident until much later in my life. However, that command made a lasting impression upon me, and was the reason why a lot of this lifetime has been spent in secret, hiding from myself, as well as from others, not able to share.

In fact, now looking back upon this lifetime, I have been very secretive regarding me, always fearful to speak out. It was as though I were playing two different roles—the secretive one, who was very much an introvert, while the other part longed to be open, loving and sharing.

However, there was always the fear of saying the wrong thing, of revealing something, but I was uncertain as to what it was I wasn't to reveal. I wasn't afraid of saying anything about that incident, for shortly after it occurred that memory was literally kicked out of my head.

Evidently I brought into this lifetime memories of a past life that should not have been there. In other words, the timing wasn't right for me to have that much awareness. Back then, they might have locked me up in an insane asylum and thrown away the key had I revealed what I remembered.

We all agree, on some level, to everything that we experience each lifetime. Since nothing happens by accident, I must have needed those experiences. Otherwise I probably would never have developed the compassion, the understanding, and especially my unconditional love, which I have gleaned through my search for me. Anyway, it was the path I chose and, as far as I am concerned, it was all worth it—more tools to work with in my service to the Light and to myself.

That message—"tell no one about this"—became, for me, the

equation that I was to be very cautious as to what I said to anyone about anything. It was like walking a tightrope, unable to share.

Of course, now there are no secrets. I have come to realize that was not the intent at all. Nevertheless, that incident did play a very important role in this lifetime. It also made me more separated, lonely and distrustful, mostly of myself. Not trusting one's own opinions can really get in the way of any happiness or success; self-doubt can be very destructive.

It wasn't long after that another incident occurred, which finalized my forgetting who I was. It also set me on the path of searching for that essence, that I somehow remembered, and had become separated from.

I was out in the pasture, some distance from the house, with my older brother. He was putting the bridle on his horse, Fancy. The other horses were busy munching grass. Jude, a large workhorse, started over toward us.

I remember watching as this scene unfolded. The big horse whirled and kicked. Its hoof connected with the back of my head with a dull thud. Blood was running down my neck as I sat there on the ground. My brother jumped on his horse and raced off to get help.

There was no pain. Everything seemed to be very clear. Sitting there, I watched as something like an essence left me. For some unexplained reason, I knew that which was leaving was a very important part of me.

There was a feeling of sadness and loneliness, which I had never been aware of having until then, but which, especially the loneliness, became constant companions. That missing essence evidently left a big vacancy within my knowingness of who I really was. Life became quite difficult from then on.

However, life does go on. Most of it, for me, was in a sort of a daze, like operating on only two cylinders instead of all twelve. School was a nightmare and a struggle, trying to fit in, but never seeming to in any area—at least in my estimation.

This was partly due to our having to move off of the farm. The Dust Bowl hit Dad hard and, after giving up farming, we moved into the little town of Norton. There was such a feeling of security while on the farm with my animals. Now I was forced to adjust to a totally different life. I was always in the lower half of my class, as far as grades were concerned, and felt so separated that school became a real struggle.

Evidently my low vibration attracted some hard taskmasters to assist me on my path—low vibration always does. I found myself often the butt of cruel remarks, which drove me further into separation and loneliness.

I had been born with an off-bite, where my lower teeth did not quite match my upper ones—a sort of a protruding jaw, which was a characteristic of my father's side of the family. This "deformity" made me feel like some kind of a freak.

I never felt pretty, for there was always that one rather small but, for me, very noticeable and "ugly" part. Thus I began hating how I looked, which only added to my feelings of insecurity.

Upon viewing some of my pictures later in my life, I discovered I was quite pretty, with a real good figure. However, I never felt pretty, and always dreamed of the day it would be corrected. Then my life would be "different," or so I thought.

Detesting that very minor imperfection so much, I later in life went to great lengths to create a partial loss of my hearing. From what the doctor said, it was caused by my "off-bite." After putting my body through two painful operations, I still wasn't happy with my looks, although the operation did correct the hearing problem.

Now I realize that it wasn't my face that needed adjusting, it was my attitude toward me. If I hadn't focused so much on that "imperfection"—wanting to be like others instead of celebrating the difference—it probably would have been a scenario, which I could have avoided. Our ego, until balanced, can blind us to the truth.

The plastic surgeons are kept quite busy trying to improve our outside appearance, when all it would take is to love ourselves, unconditionally, as we are. Nothing will change our own perception of how we look until we do. When we change our perception of ourselves, then others will also see us in a new light. If they don't, it won't matter—not when we love ourselves, unconditionally.

My fifth grade teacher assisted me greatly in my own reflections of being less than nothing. One day she spanked me for not having my homework done. I had been ill, and had missed school the day before. So I wasn't aware of the assignment. This she did with great delight, in front of the class.

Shortly after that episode, she asked me to tell her my middle name, which is Blanche. I'm certain she already knew and was baiting me, for when I told her she immediately retorted, "Oh that rhymes with branch, which I can use to spank you again."

Of course, she said it in front of the whole class. I wanted to disappear under my desk in my embarrassment, as they all laughed at her cruel "joke." She really must have been hurting, and it must have given her some kind of relief to hurt a vulnerable child in that way. If we are hurting, we then will strike out at others, sometimes in very destructive ways.

Another time, she pulled me up in front of the class. Making me stand before those to whom I already felt so very inferior, she showed them how my teeth didn't fit properly together. When I told Mother, she went to the school and really blasted her.

Ms. Shepherd pretty much cooled it after that. However, my ego was so deflated by then that I kept pretty much to myself. I can't recall having any positive self-identification, so began taking on false personalities in order to survive.

Life continued being a blur. We were in the middle of a depression, so had to move around a lot. Dad was doing whatever he could to make a living for the family. It must have been really hard on him, giving up farming. The Dust Bowl had wiped him out.

I can remember him telling me that I had a "hop-toad mind," which made me feel even less acceptable, if that were possible. Now I can see that he was seeing his own reflection. However, at that time there was no way of sorting that one out, so I accepted the cruel fact of being neither pretty nor smart.

Then, wonder of wonders, at sweet sixteen I was introduced to the so-called fun and glamour of doing and becoming like my big sister. She was, to me, everything I wasn't and wanted to be, and so I really worked on perfecting a false personality.

Little did I know that she was also blindly trying to find her own self-identification, covering up her insecurities by drinking, being the life of the party, and cheating on her husband.

While living with them during my senior year of high school, I met a young man, Red. He was old enough to drink, so I joined him, partying half the night and trying to fathom my studies enough to graduate.

After graduation, I went back home to Papa and Mother, bolstered up with my new personality and hiding that lost, scared, lonely little girl from everyone, including myself.

The war had begun—the war to end all wars—what a cosmic joke that was. I went to work making bullets so that people could be killed, and spent my money on parties and booze.

My sister-in-law introduced me to a man quite a lot older and far worldlier than I, and so I no longer remained a virgin. I always wanted to "go all the way," but always stopped short, due to those old religious beliefs. However, there had been a lot of heavy petting with Red during my senior year.

That felt good, but this was great, or so I thought. It was usually almost over before it had begun. Heavy, hot foreplay and then wham, bam—thank you, ma'am. Later he told me he was getting married, and we would have to break our relationship off. My ego was crushed, I wasn't. I was incapable of love then.

Red returned from the war, and asked me to marry him. So, not having anything better to do, I said yes. Now that was about as much thought or feeling that I was capable of having at that time. And so we were married, which I enjoyed for a while—mostly because of the attention from him, and of being a new bride.

We had a baby girl born to us. She was a beautiful baby. Being a new mother took up a lot of my time and made me feel happy and content, for a while. However, again I started feeling something was missing out of my life. This started me reaching outside of myself, and the marriage bed in order to satisfy that deep longing of finding that missing part of me. I, of course, went searching in all the wrong places— drinking and other men.

Red was a good old boy—loyal, steadfast, worked to support us, and never read me "the riot act." Did I appreciate him? Not one bit. Evidently there just wasn't enough turmoil in my life—not enough action. Divorcing him, I took our little three-year-old girl, Sharon, and again went to live with my sister and her husband.

Red never seemed to object or stand up for himself in any way. He must have been as fogged up as I. There was no spiritual vibration between us, just two bodies coming together. Evidently that was enough for him, but not for me.

So once again I was reaching outside of myself for that certain connection and didn't have a clue as to what. It was like a burning desire, driving me on in search of fulfillment.

My sister and her husband were drifting further apart. It's laughable, but true how I tried, in my own confused way, to counsel them. As the old saying goes, one tries to teach what one needs to learn themselves.

The time spent with them was more or less a blur. I drank and partied a lot, leaving my little three-year-old baby girl alone, locked up in my bedroom.

Believe me, I have spent some very remorseful and unnerving hours wondering what she must have gone through. Did she wake up while I was gone? Was she frightened, crying, all alone in a big room with no one there to comfort her?

I'm certain of one thing and that is, if given the chance to relive that time, there would be no way that I would even think of repeating those kind of actions. I now have the capability to love and nurture myself. In doing so, I would now also be able to do the same for others, especially my children.

I returned home with Sharon to Papa and Mother, which was a good thing, for this was their only grandchild and she was the "apple of their eye." They gave her the attention and love that I was incapable of at that time, for which I am very thankful.

She never went hungry, was always kept clean, and I did play with her a lot. However, it wasn't the full-time attention that she deserved. Yes, I have had many regrets regarding her early childhood.

However, I am no longer condemning myself, but have now blessed those experiences and let them go. Turning my life completely around has given me the opportunity to assist her and others in a positive way.

Judging and beating oneself up over the past is not very commendable.

It only perpetuates and feeds that negative energy. As we all know, the past is the past. One can't change what was, but one can make certain they don't repeat those actions through the lessons learned.

At Papa's insistence, I remarried Red. Back then males, if they were at all strong-willed—which Papa was the epitome of—could and did override my own weak desires. After all, who was I to demand or express what I wanted, and the big question was "What did I really want?"

I doubt if Papa would have understood for he was not very understanding of feelings, especially of the female. Why else would I have chosen him for a father. He was a great reflection, for at that time I had neither understanding nor compassion for myself.

So once again I found myself, secretly reluctant, but nevertheless saying "I do," and felt the door of freedom being slammed shut again. Why Red remarried me is a mystery. Evidently he was as mixed up as I, and was also searching for that illusive butterfly. He certainly found one in me, for he always put up with whatever I dished out.

We had a darling baby boy, Jimmy. This settled me down for a while, but soon I was off and running again, chasing after my own "illusive butterfly."

Having sex outside of the marriage bed seemed, at that time, to be more of a challenge. There never seemed to be any guilt regarding my actions. If there was, they had been buried with all of my other feelings. At that time, the only true feelings I had were sexual and loneliness. The rest of me was really shut down.

I finally divorced Red, I'm not certain on what grounds, without a thought as to his feelings. I now recall how hurt and confused he was.

I had met a man twenty years older than I. He was an alcoholic, a "devil on wheels", and was everything Red wasn't. He didn't work a lot of the time, would go totally crazy when he drank, and made my life a living hell, along with Jimmy's and Sharon's.

I didn't seem to be aware at that time of what I was doing. You might liken me to a leaf being blown by the wind. I didn't seem to know or care where I landed, nor did I ever give a thought as to the consequences therein for either my children or myself.

I neither loved nor took responsibility for myself—whoever that was. Since there was no love for myself, there was no way I could either love or be responsible for anyone else.

If I was searching for me—my essence—at that time, then whatever I was doing never worked. The part of me that had left so many years ago was no place around. It would take much more searching, and in a totally different area, before I would be united with it again.

The older man's name was Mac. When he was drunk, he would go completely berserk, threatening to kill the kids. This would bring out the protective mother instinct in me and I would go head-on with him.

He was much larger than I, but I was more powerful, not physically, but more agile, both mentally and physically. He usually ended up the loser, but I never escaped unscathed. I had my share of black eyes, broken ribs, et cetera. Perhaps all of this was a sort of payback karma for the way I treated Red.

Evidently there was some kind of relief we received from these confrontations, for I did, in my own unique way, co-create, them. We both had tons of pent-up anger and guilt just waiting to explode, and so we used each other to release it. From my observation and experience I believe this is why so many, especially women, put up with physical abuse, because of their self-guilt. Of course, the alcohol, which we both indulged in, did add fuel to the fire.

Looking back, I now realize the reason I put up with it for so long. It was a sort of self-punishment for my guilt feelings. There was always that feeling of being guilty, but for what I didn't know. All I knew was that I had done something that was unforgivable, thus creating scenarios for which I could be punished. My sub-conscious probably created those scenarios in order to uncover that dastardly deed I somehow felt responsible for, hidden some place in my distant past.

Mac was a master at assisting me in this. He would beat me up. Then, after he was sober, he would treat me like a child, caring for my black eyes and bruises. And, because of my deep need for love and my constant guilt feelings, I was grateful for that attention. This was really a sick game, but it did serve a purpose in a weird sort of way.

Having worked all the time, I had my own car. He worked some, and of all places, as a bartender. I recall one time when he bought a car. I had gotten him out of the house and he was living elsewhere.

He showed up one early morning, drunk. I was trying to get the kids off to school. "Come take a drive with me," he demanded belligerently. "I want to show you my new car."

"I can't, I've got to get the kids off to school." I stalled, trying to keep the fear out of my voice.

This seemed to anger him even more, so I decided to make a deal with him by saying, "Well, if you'll drop the kids off at school, I'll go with you." I knew that this way they would be safe from his drunken temper—I never knew when it might explode.

This he agreed to do. So, after dropping the kids off, we headed for the mountains. He seemed to be getting great pleasure out of scaring me half to death by driving real fast around dangerous mountain curves. I wasn't certain whether we were going to make some of them or not. I was playing the part of a victim, big time, and didn't like it.

Then a plan started forming. I'd get the keys from him and drive. "Gee, this is really a nice car," I said. "How about letting me drive?"

This seemed to please him. "Sure," he replied, stopping the car. I climbed into the driver's seat and he into the passenger side, handing me the keys.

We drove into a little mountain town and came upon a tavern. "Pull in here, I need a drink," he ordered. I played along with his mood and pulled in.

We went inside and he ordered a drink, and was insisting that I join him.

"Come on," the bartender said. "Why not? What's the harm?"

Knowing how alcohol affected me, I didn't dare take that drink. I had to keep my wits about me if I were to extricate myself from this situation I was in.

Then, remembering that there was a ladies' restroom near the tavern's entrance, I said, "Okay, pour me one while I go visit the little girls' room."

Mac evidently had forgotten that I had the keys, so let me go. I quickly made my way to the car and drove off.

I'll never forget the dumbfounded look on his face in the rearview mirror as he watched me drive away. Evidently he had come looking for me, probably remembering that I had the keys. Chalk one up for me. He showed up much later, sober, so I gave him back his keys.

There were many traumatic scenarios during our life together. One of which was when he came home from a night of drinking. He had wanted me to go with him, but I was taking longer to dress than he thought I should, so off to the bars he went without me.

He came back in a drunken rage. He upset the refrigerator, food spilling out all over the floor. Then, charging into the living room, he waltzed the piano across the floor but couldn't upset it. So he came after me. Running to the kitchen, I picked up the heavy lid of a pressure cooker, and let him have it with all of my might. He left, blood dripping from his head, but not until he had twisted my thumb, almost breaking it.

I don't recall whether Shari and Jimmy were with me or at my parents' that night. I pray it was the latter, for that was really a night to remember.

These games continued on for some time. I paid for three different divorces before finally letting it go through. Evidently I still felt the need to be punished. I couldn't have picked a better person for this sick need of mine. He was perfect in every way.

Before my final divorce, there was one more episode where I came out unscathed, but he didn't. He was drunk and decided to have sex with me, so he came to the home I had bought. I had taken on a roommate and her little boy to help with expenses.

First, he knelt in front of the large window, pleading. I said, "Get lost or I'm calling the police." This only made him angry. Jerking the window open, he started climbing through it. Poor little Rena was scared spitless.

He had gotten his head and shoulders through the opening, and I knew something had to be done. So, grabbing my son's .22 rifle, I hit him over the head with the butt end. He must have had a very hard head, for it cracked the wood on the butt of that gun.

He left, holding his head and moaning. I was not bothered any more by him. Sometime later he died of a heart attack. Would I have gone back to him again had he not died? This I will never know.

However, I do know that now I wouldn't even give him a second glance. I love myself too much to place either myself or my children in that kind of a scenario ever again.

Why did I continue allowing this to go on? Well, for one thing, back then there was always that feeling of having done something unforgivable, but not knowing what it was. And, of course, not loving myself brought on the feeling of undeserving—this is prevalent in many of us.

However, once realizing the reason for creating such self-destructive scenarios, I have been able to release my self-judgments, and choose more wisely a path of higher vibration. Thus the need to punish myself no longer exists.

I evidently kept on creating scenarios that would be difficult to forgive, probably in order to unlock those long forgotten judgments and bring them to the surface. Once recognized, our judgments of what we have done can then be removed from the subconscious mind, allowing us to live in the present, not the past. Now I love myself unconditionally, so have no need to place myself within such scenarios ever again.

We create negative scenarios, subconsciously, in order to bring forth our stuff so we can release it. Thus, when our judgments have been released, we free ourselves from those tormenting and destructive guilt feelings. The need to punish ourselves and others no longer exists. We then forgive and love ourselves and others unconditionally. This is when we stop creating those hurtful and harmful scenarios, for ourselves and others. This, my friend, is true freedom.

Many a time I wanted to end it all—contemplating suicide, speeding around mountain curves, hoping I wouldn't make it, but never really following through on any of it.

Many of you probably have, in your own way, been in that state of mind—wanting to escape from either a situation, or from that part of yourself that you no longer want to face. It's never the whole one tries to escape from, only that part which seems insurmountable.

The real victims were Shari and Jimmy, for they were the ones who were scared and upset. They were little children, huddling together, not knowing what to do or who to turn to.

Later I learned that they would make plans to run away, but never carried them out. This, of course, shaped their lives, for the path they chose to walk this lifetime with me during those formative young years was very traumatic.

However, we each choose the path that will give us what we need for our own expansion and growth. I did, they did, we all do. None of us are victims. We are powerful spirits in bodies—learning, experiencing and evolving into more of who we are.

I married one more time and, yes, to another alcoholic. Jimmy and Shari had both left and were on their own paths, searching for their own identity and, of course, looking in all the wrong places, following in my footsteps.

Life with Glen was not nearly as traumatic—he was more of a happy drunk. Still, I was not happy. Evidently my Higher Self knew this, for I finally set myself free from him. It was through him that I was led to The Church of Scientology, and started digging my way out of the fog that I had been in during this and other lifetimes.

We both were trying to find ourselves through Scientology auditing. It wasn't apparent to me why I couldn't stand being with him, for he was a prince compared to Mac. Of course, he did drink a lot, periodically, which probably restimulated my memories of my past traumatic encounters. I did go into fear when he drank.

I now have a clearer picture of the reasons and it had very little to do with those episodes. Yes, it did have some effect. However, the biggest bug-a-boo was that we had shared another lifetime, where it ended up that I killed him, blaming him for what we had co-created.

It's so easy to blame others for our own creations, judging the scenario as "bad." That is how we get ourselves stuck in past incidents— through our judgments. This then will lead to ungrounded fears that somehow they will find out and will "get even." So we "get them before they get us." Of course, unless we are very aware, this is all played out without any idea of why, creating more confusion. Fear is always the bottom line.

Evidently we came together this lifetime for closure of that unhappy one, which I have done. He was a good reflection for me at that time, but now, like the saying "I've already done that, so thanks, but no thanks—I no longer need those kinds of reflections.

He had gone through several shock treatments this lifetime before I met him, and sent out some pretty weird vibes or thoughts. Being very empathic, which I wasn't aware of until much later, I would pick them up. Not knowing exactly what was happening or what to do with those thoughts, I would sometimes do crazy things trying to escape from them. His thoughts, combined with my own, along with that hidden past-life scenario, were very unbalancing. His drinking didn't help any either, for it always made me more fearful, thus trapping me in my fear.

Fear, which is always the bottom line for why we react in a negative way, would come up when he drank—probably a combination of his and mine. He would threaten, but was never really violent. I couldn't handle it then. I could now. In fact, if I had known then what I know now, our ending might have been completely different.

Shortly after divorcing him, he committed suicide in one of his drinking escapades. Finally I was free from the entanglements of feeling any need for someone to make me feel whole. I wasn't certain where I was going, but knew that Scientology was, at that time, for me. My kids were grown and on their own, and had been for some time.

There was a kind of knowingness within me, thanks to the guidance of my Higher Soul Self and my Guides and Angels, that I was going to find that missing part of me.

Since I had always worked and supported my kids, my two drunken husbands and myself, I had neither doubts nor fears in being able to survive. So eagerly I began exploring the many-faceted me, which would reveal the yet unanswered questions of why I acted the way I did. Why I couldn't really love or accept being loved.

Love, not for others but for myself, was the missing essence for which I longed and somehow had an inner knowingness that until I was united with It once more, I would never feel complete or whole. This new journey was to lead me to the answer of my yet unanswered question, WHO AM I?

The feelings of Fear and Excitement
are exactly the same vibration
until judged

HOWEVER
when judged
Fear will send you plunging down
into Illusion's dark
Abyss

Excitement will send you soaring into
higher realms of creativity

ETS, SPACESHIPS AND OTHER
"OUT OF WORLD" PHENOMENA

Star People, Earth People, what is in a name?
Look past the illusion, for we are all the same
Star People, Earth People, together we will fly
As our hands touch yours in friendship
Connecting planets, earth and sky

I have always had a deep inner knowingness that there were other forms of life similar to ours, yet more highly evolved, and with greater love and compassion than we have ever experienced here on planet Earth. I was right.

My journey in the search for my missing essence this lifetime led me on many an exciting excursion. Some of these sent me spinning into other worlds, allowing me to connect with others, who were not in this third-dimensional existence. This, I am happy to say, was without the assistance of hallucinating or hypnotic drugs.

I can never remember a time that I didn't wish for, searched the skies for, and even sometimes felt that a spaceship or something was close by—yet not quite within my physical sight. This left me sometimes doubting my own sanity and knowingness.

My first real step in finding the true me was when I was led to Scientology. This was long before discovering The Awakenings, in New Mexico. I don't question why I didn't leap right into The Awakenings. It probably was because they had not been established on the planet at that time and, also, the timing wasn't right—TIMING IS EVERYTHING.

I look upon each step taken as the right experience for me at any given time—as it is for each of us. True, it cost me a lot of money. However, the opening of my memory to the extent that it did was priceless. In fact, the data gleaned from their teachings I still use—after all, you don't throw the baby out with the bath water.

Scientology had a tremendous amount of usable technology. However, it was more mental than heart and, as the song goes, you've got to have heart. One thing it did was to reach into and open up my memory banks, exposing past traumatic experiences and judgments, thus setting me on the right path of finding me.

The Scientology Auditor acts as a guide, monitoring reactions by using an E Meter, something akin to a lie detector, yet far more effective and accurate. This was accomplished with certain key questions or words. Suddenly, a whole lifetime would open up, not all at once, but gradually. This would then start jogging my memory, which, in turn, would open up more of my memory of past lives, some of which became very clear.

The Auditors never told me what was going on. How could they, for they didn't have a clue. Their only job was to guide me into the dark abyss of my hidden past. They are trained to watch the needle; which is very accurate in indicating when one has arrived, or is getting close to some so-called "dastardly deed."

Our memories of other lifetimes hold the truth of the powerful beings we truly are. These we have locked away in the dark alcoves of our minds in order not to face whatever we have judged, or have refused to take responsibility for.

It is sort of a game we have created that "I'll hide whatever I don't want to face, in order not to feel responsible or be blamed for. Then no one will ever know about them, even myself." Believe me, some of those memories are very traumatic, dying, being born, losing loved ones, killing, torturing, the list goes on and on. Oh yes, we have all played on both sides of the polarities. Some we probably would prefer never to face, let alone claim that we were in any way responsible.

The truth is nothing is bad. All is for our own and our co-creators' experience and evolvement. It is only when we judge the action as bad is when it becomes so. We then proceed to hide it from others as well as ourselves, locking it safely away within the most inaccessible confines of our mind—safely hidden from everyone's view, or so we believe.

However, in doing so we also hide the good, forgetting everything, thus poor memory and forgetfulness occurs. When I became willing to look at everything, it was like unlocking a door that led through a maze of different stories which wove a thread connecting me to past lifetimes, and I was the main actor in each.

This truly was, for me, a fascinating ride. By opening the doors of my past, I discovered why I continued repeatedly doing certain things that caused me not to get ahead, either on the spiritual or earthly plane.

So I traveled the amazing maze of my many lives through auditing, remembering, taking off layers of judgment, pain and guilt. It was on the very highest level of what Scientology had to offer, NOTS, when I became aware that I still wasn't finding my true essence which had been separated from me by that kick and had long departed.

I now know that which left me was my own signature vibration, which is love, especially love for myself. This left me with only a ghost of a memory of that love whose haunting voice kept calling me, urging me on and on.

I finally realized that their missing ingredient was the same one that I was missing—Love. It really is a cosmic joke that we are drawn to others who are reflecting the same missing ingredient that we are searching for, even when we, on this level, don't at the time have a clue as to why we are amongst them.

Finally separating from the Scientology church with a letter of resignation, but keeping all that I had learned from that experience, again I found myself looking for that illusive Holy Grail. So named, for it is what we all are searching for—something that will release us from that burning thirst, which drives us blindly on and on, and give meaning to our empty lives.

Had I known back then that all answers lie within each of us, I could have shortened my search considerably. But, of course, that wasn't to be. Besides, I might not have had the fantastic privilege of experiencing all the wonderful surprises that lay in store for me.

Now I realize that, inch by inch, step by step, we draw nearer and nearer to total Self-realization until, finally, we find ourselves soaring out of Illusion's trap. It's not the journey's end, but the journey itself that makes life so very interesting. After leaving Scientology, I felt like the rug had just been pulled out from under me and was wondering where I would land next.

I didn't have long to wait, for shortly thereafter, I received a call from Bruce, a friend of mine who had also disconnected from Scientology. "I just got a call from Steve Muro. He's found something that he believes we would find interesting. Want to come along?" he asked.

Steve was a mutual friend and also a former Scientologist. No longer under the protective, controlling umbrella of Scientology and at loose ends, I jumped at the chance. In fact, for some reason I felt a thrill of excitement run through me. Little did I know just how deeply this would affect my life.

Bashar—A Messenger from Outer Space:

Bruce picked me up, but for some reason didn't connect with Bashar the way I did. Evidently he "was out to lunch" that day. I however, unlike him, felt a great sensation of love and joy when Bashar entered Darryl Anka's body. Darryl was the channel for Bashar—a space brother from the planet, Essassani, which is located outside of our solar system.

There was an instant knowingness saying, "This is for me." I was vibrating at a far higher level of excitement than I could ever remember. It was as though a door was opening through which an old forgotten friend was about to enter.

The knowledge and the love that poured forth from that wonderful Being of Light was the answer to my prayer. Talk about opening up one's awareness, boy, did he ever! I continued attending at least once to twice a week. First, there were only a few of us, for Darryl had just started channeling Bashar.

We met at Steve's small home in North Hollywood. However, word got around and soon we were sitting on each other's laps, the floor, or any place else we could find. All of us were eager to hear his wonderful messages, expanding our awareness and drinking in that fantastic love vibration which was a part of Bashar's essence. I attended every session and felt I was on a roll.

He would cover many subjects regarding life on Essassani, spaceships, and other galaxies. When he talked about the Sirius star system, there was such a beautiful feeling that I knew I had been there. It felt so familiar, almost like the home I kept longing for but never was able to find.

No question was ever judged. He treated each of us with love, understanding, and answered our eager questions about other life forms, other planets, as well as what was happening as far as our evolvement on planet Earth. It was a trip I will never forget, and will always be grateful for.

Close Encounters:

Many things happened to and for me at that time. I had my first memory of my encounter with my Whole Soul Self where She/He gave me Its name—MeAmba. True, I did have a fantastic experience a few years earlier. It happened during an auditing session in Scientology.

Sitting in front of the auditor, holding the E-Meter cans, the next thing I knew I had exploded out of my body. No longer was I on Earth. I still had a body, but what a body, it was huge—much larger than Earth. I remember looking down and seeing planets entering and passing through me. There was no fear—in fact, there didn't seem to be much feeling at all. It felt so natural, like any reoccurring incident we experience here on Earth every day. Then it was over as quickly as it had begun, and I was back in my physical body again.

"What happened?" the auditor asked, for she didn't have a clue, except that the E-Meter had really been talking to her.

"I really don't know," I replied, trying to explain the incident. She wrote down what I told her and it was never mentioned again. What would I tell her if this happened now? I probably would nonchalantly say, "Oh, I just entered my seventh-dimensional Higher Soul Self," lay down the cans and walk out, never to return, but that was then and this is now.

However, this time it was a completely different experience, more on an earthly level. I was walking one Sunday afternoon up above Glendale, California, which was my home. It was a lovely area with mountains and trees.

I had just experienced an exciting moment, while walking up the mountain, of an encounter with fear. It wasn't very large, nor dense— more like a shadow, making its presence known in a strange way by sending a cold shiver up the middle of my spine.

Turning around, I saw this dark shape sort of following me. Remembering Bashar's talk on handling fear by confronting it head-on, I lovingly asked, "Would you like to join me?" Suddenly the dark shadow became very light and disappeared, leaving only a joyful feeling, and the chill left. This is a wonderful way to handle any negativity—face it with love, without judgment, for love is the most powerful of all.

I continued up the mountain. Then, suddenly, a bushy tree started really shaking. I stopped, fascinated. I remember thinking, "Moses saw a burning bush. Perhaps this was God's way of getting a message through to me."

However, it wasn't anything quite as dramatic as that, for just then a deer stuck his head through the bush. He had a wonderful rack of horns and big, soulful eyes. It was so close that I could have reached out and touched its nose. I gazed into those beautiful eyes for a moment. Then, with another shaking of the branches, it disappeared, leaving me with a feeling of high excitement.

As I joyously skipped down the mountain, I heard the name MeAmba. It kept coming to me, like a whisper. I suddenly became aware that was the name of my Whole Soul Self from the seventh dimension. I had never been aware of this Being's existence until that moment, and I have never been unaware of Her/His existence since.

41

Ah, yes, Spirit does act in wondrous ways. All we have to do is be open to receiving the gifts. As Bashar always said, "Believing is seeing, not the other way around." Did the deer have anything to do with the message? It is my belief that it did—that it was a sort of messenger raising my vibration so that I was aware enough to receive it. Our animals are such wonderful guides, both here and in the spirit world.

Soon after that, I went to visit my brother, who lived at the Cays just outside of Coronado Beach. It was late afternoon. I decided to go down and walk the beach and find some shells. There was no one but myself on the beach, which struck me as being odd, for usually many were down there enjoying the water and the late afternoon sun.

I walked along the water's edge, picking up sand dollars and other shells, not thinking of anything in particular—just enjoying the moment. Suddenly, it felt as though I was being bathed in some kind of a warm, beautiful glow.

It was almost the same kind of feeling I had felt on my first encounter with Bashar, only much stronger, more loving—words are so inadequate when one tries to describe emotions.

My body was really vibrating with excitement. Then I got the thought or message to look up. I did, and to my astonishment saw a huge triangular ship floating just above the ocean. It appeared to be made of some kind of metallic material and had a sort of translucent glow—which could have been caused by the sun's rays reflecting off of it.

I stood, entranced, not able to move, saying over and over, "Thank you, thank you," as tears of joy ran down my cheeks. Then, without a sound, it shot back over the ocean and disappeared as quickly as it had appeared. What a memorable and exciting moment that was. I was so high that I almost flew back to the house.

This happened on a Friday evening. I attended another Bashar meeting on Sunday, and again I didn't share or say anything to anyone about my encounter. I wanted to, but evidently that command I received as a small child still was controlling me, so I kept silent.

A group of my friends were discussing seeing the same thing at Malibu Beach, outside of Los Angeles, as I had seen down at Coronado Beach, outside of San Diego. Upon asking Bashar during our meeting, he said that he had brought his ship into our area.

Later, Bashar took us up into his spaceship. We each went to different areas. I remember going into a room which held a giant crystal sphere. It was glowing with shimmering crystals of many colors, and was so beautiful it almost took my breath away.

Upon returning and while sharing what we had experienced, Bashar told us that this was their transmitting area. They transmit thought, using crystals, in the same way as we do words via telephone. They are far more advanced, telepathically using thought concepts in place of words.

I also visited a huge area with trees, plants, and other vegetation. Evidently that was where they raised their food for the ship. Some told about visiting a sort of kitchen, where their food is prepared, while others visited their recreation and other areas. I felt, and still do, so very privileged to have had that wonderful encounter and to experience the love that they showered upon me.

What a difference from some of the horror stories others have experienced in their encounters with the not-so-nice ETs. Yes, there are both kinds out there. Bashar has talked to us about them. The main thing is to raise our vibration so high that those ETs, who are in a lower vibration, are not even aware that we exist.

Once we are really in the high vibration of Unconditional Love, then nothing can penetrate that wondrous shield of protection. How do we arrive at that high vibration? The best advice I can give is to love unconditionally with no judgment, beginning with self.

This will, automatically, spread to loving everything and everybody equally—the higher your vibration, the more protected you will be from the effects of lower vibrations. Vibrating in the higher frequencies will also allow us to see beyond the "physical" into other worlds, such as space ships, ETs and other realms. Since love is the highest vibration of all, the more we love. the higher our vibration.

Love frees you, judgment traps you within its negativity of whatever you are judging, thus lowering your vibration. I, of course, raised mine through The Awakenings.

Bashar taught me so many things and, at times, I still can feel his wonderful presence. What a beautiful blessing he has been to me, as well as to others. His message was love—the very essence for which so very long I had been searching. Thank you, my beautiful friend, for coming and assisting me in recognizing my true essence. I love you and you will always be a part of me forever.

Turning the Dark to Light—An ET's Visit:

This encounter happened up in the Idyllwild area. Idyllwild is a beautiful, mystical little mountain town located high above Palm Springs, California. I had gone up to spend the weekend with my son, Jimmy. We had taken his little camper back into the forest, camping near a stream.

Jimmy had gone to bed and was sound asleep. I had been asleep, but was now wide awake and wasn't sure why. Suddenly I felt compelled to get up and go to the door. Opening the door of the little camper, there, directly in front of me, was someone in what looked like a white spacesuit.

He had a sort of glow about him, but I couldn't quite distinguish his features. I started to speak and was aware that there was no fear, just a sort of inquisitive feeling. However, he held up his hand and I got the message, "Not now." Then he left.

I stood there, trying to decide whether to step outside or not. It was quite dark with trees casting weird shadows upon the mountain. And, as usual, a feeling of fear shot through me—there had always been some fear of darkness within me.

Suddenly the whole forest seemed to light up around the little camper. I softly called Thor and he came. He had not made a sound, a bark, a growl—nothing, which was unusual for him, for he was a Doberman-Rottweiler and had been trained to be a watchdog.

I stepped out of the little camper with Thor close beside me and we walked up the mountain trail, which also was as bright as day. I wanted to get another glimpse of this night visitor, but he never returned. I really hope that someday he will, for I have a few hundred questions to ask him.

One thing I do know is that I have never feared the dark since that night. Whatever happened between us in that brief encounter was, to say the least, magical.

Parallel Worlds, Indians, and Buried Treasure:

It all started when I was reading an article in the local paper while sitting in my Phoenix home. It was telling an Indian folklore of a buried treasure, which, for some reason, gave my memory a jolt. The article was saying something about some treasure being buried "under the old Indian's nose."

I thought no more about it until not long after a picture appeared in the same paper of someone jumping from one huge rock to another somewhere in the Sedona area. Now the rocks she was jumping across didn't seem to hold much interest for me. However, there was a rock in the background with the face of an Indian—big nose and all.

That is when a scene began to unfold. It was like sitting in front of a movie screen and watching yourself being portrayed in another lifetime. There I was, an Indian warrior on a horse, with a group of Indians who were also on horses. We were silently waiting, watching, hiding behind some large rocks.

Suddenly a wagon, accompanied by six or eight soldiers dressed in blue uniforms, appeared. Silently we waited and just as the wagon was almost directly across from us, we attacked. There wasn't much of a skirmish. The soldiers lay dead on the ground, and we were taking oblong gold bars from the wagon, putting them on the backs of our horses.

As I came back to present time and Planet Earth, I felt that I knew just where this had taken place, and where the gold had been buried.

While living in Phoenix, I had traveled many times up to Sedona. Sometimes I would stop in Cottonwood on my way up, and visit with a friend of mine and her boyfriend, who was half-Indian. Jumping in my car, off I sped to tell them of my vision. I felt certain that I could lead them to the Indian rock where the treasure had been taken and buried.

They were very excited, so off we went. Parking the car, we started walking. The trail, which at first was rather easy, soon became narrow and steep. Still we were determined to find that cave so pushed on, even though none of us really knew where we were going. Looking back on it now, it was more or less like the blind leading the blind.

Yet, for some reason, we felt that somehow we were being guided. But by whom or what we hadn't a clue. As we came down a rather steep incline, I looked up and there, just above me, was a cave with a huge rock standing like a sentinel in front of it.

"That's it!" I said excitedly, pointing to the cave and the rock. "I remember that rock being in front of the cave. And there is the Indian's big nose just above it." We hurried up to where it was. The cave was very dark inside.

By now it was getting almost sunset, so we decided to go back and return the next day. I needed more durable clothes if we were going to crawl through caves. So, as agreed, we met the next day. This time we drove much closer to the cave for we had discovered that a road had been built not too far above it.

For two weeks we dug, dynamited, literally tearing the cave apart. We came to an opening where we could stand. The cave had a ledge running along its wall. I put my hand up and felt, expecting any minute to touch the deer skin pouches that the gold had been wrapped in. Instead, I felt round holes and knew that we had set our torches there in order to see. "We're getting close," I told them. "It's in a sort of round-like room, and this ledge is also part of that room."

Now we were really excited and the tiredness I had felt dropped away. But the cave seemed to have come to a dead end. We tried blasting with more dynamite, but it was like granite. We went outside and I decided to withdraw and take another look at this vision.

Seating myself down the hill a little ways, with my back against a big juniper, I tried recalling the exact vision, thinking perhaps it would open up more of that scenario for me.

I glanced up above the cave where the rock with the face of the Indian with his big nose jutted out. Then I stared in total amazement, for standing on the rock above the cave and just below the Indian rock was an Indian chief dressed in full regalia—war bonnet and all.

We both just stood there, looking at each other, caught up in another time warp. Then he vanished, as quickly as he had appeared. Excited, I ran up to where my friends were and told them what I had seen. I also told them that no further information regarding the treasure had come to me. So, for several more days, we tried to break through that granite wall, but to no avail.

I did get some sort of information that Union soldiers had blasted many caves shut in that area in order to prohibit the Indians from hiding in them. Finally, after several more attempts at breaking through that wall, and seeing the old chief several more times, we decided that we might as well admit defeat. Loading our camping gear and shovels in the car, we said goodbye to that adventure and went back to the humdrum everyday existence of our lives.

Not long after that, I decided to move to California. But before doing so, I found myself driving up for one last look at the cave and perhaps get one last glimpse of the old chief. I felt such a kinship toward him.

I hadn't quite reached that area when I got the message to stop the car, get out and look up on the hill above me. This was shortly after I had gone through the town of Cottonwood. I did so and, to my astonishment, the most wondrous of scenes appeared before my eyes.

There on that hill not only was the old Indian chief, but his warriors in war paint with their horses, Indian women and children, all dressed in their finest—the whole tribe was standing there silently waiting.

I felt so much a part of them, for I knew that they had come to tell me goodbye and that they were my tribe, my family. There also was a feeling of sadness at having to leave them. But life goes on and I knew I couldn't join the world that had been ours and now was theirs.

Thanking them for honoring me with their appearance, I turned my car around and headed back to Phoenix, a little shaken, awed, and very grateful for that special moment with my tribe with whom I had once shared so much.

Perhaps it was the old Indian chief who was guiding us to that cave—who knows? One thing is for certain, parallel worlds do exist and are all around us.

Releasing Earth-bound Spirits:

I have had quite a few experiences with releasing earth-bound spirits who have not yet gone on, but have somehow gotten stuck here on this third-dimensional plane. One of which vividly comes to mind was when I was in New Mexico. I had decided to go up to the hot springs some distance above Los Alamos, which holds a lot of negativity.

I chose not to take that negativity on, at least then. So I continued on my way to the springs. After a wonderful bath, I decided to by-pass Los Alamos and take another route home. At the time I wasn't certain why I had made that decision, but had traveled only a short distance when it became quite clear.

It was rather mountainous, and I was happily enjoying the beauty of trees and streams. I came upon a little valley with a stream running through it. Suddenly a chill ran up my spine, as a deep sadness engulfed me. Stopping the car I got out, and became aware of a covered wagon near the stream. A man, a woman and three children, a boy and two little girls, were there. They seemed to have been stuck in that time frame and were unable to get out of it.

Quickly I took out my crystal pendulum, which I carry with me. Calling on the Angels/Masters of Light, I began releasing the energy. There was no resistance to leaving, just a joyous sort of a golden light around them, and the whole scene disappeared. Later I was told that they had been killed by renegade Indians, and had somehow gotten stuck, unable to go on.

When I returned to my car, the chill and the sadness had completely disappeared. So I continued on down to the highway that led back to Santa Fe and home.

I did go back to Los Alamos later, and with the help of my trusted generator quartz crystal released a lot of negative energy, replacing it with love and light. A few days later there was a large article in the local paper exposing the government's mishandling of the nuclear waste in that area. This started the proceedings of cleaning it up. Did my trip up there prior to that article have anything to do with it? I'd like to think so. I do know that Spirit does act in mysterious and wondrous ways.

Another memorable time happened after I had moved to Paonia, Colorado. My little 85-year-old friend, Aurora, and I had gone to hear a channeling in Delta. We had taken off our coats and I was getting a glass of punch for her. Looking up from the punch bowl, I saw that she was leaning against the wall, her face as white as chalk.

I walked over and asked her what was happening. She seemed dazed and started talking in some language I couldn't understand. The channeling was just getting ready to start, so I took her into a bedroom and began working with her. It was as if she were being taken over by someone or something.

The lady who was going to channel came in, along with another friend of Aurora's and mine. She wanted to take her to the hospital, but I decided to take her in my car away from the house.

After driving a short distance, I stopped the car, and called in Aurora's Higher Self and Angels, as well as mine. Then, using my crystal pendulum, I lovingly asked that the entity leave. A blue light began to appear, and I saw the spirit being carried upward, away from Aurora. Together we watched it as it disappeared into the sky surrounded by the blue light.

Aurora was once again herself, bright-eyed and laughing. She looked great, so we returned to the channeling. While we were gone, the lady who was doing the channeling had gotten the information that a young Indian girl had died in that area many years before, and had gotten stuck in this dimension.

Evidently she had seen Aurora's light—which was a very bright one—and so she went for it, thus sticking herself to Aurora. But, as they say, all is well that ends well. We all had a memorable experience and a spirit was released to the light.

However, some entities are not so willing to leave, especially when they are not really of the light, but have been created through fear, hate and anger. As far as I can determine, they seem to be soul-less. I have encountered some of which I will speak of later.

Also, some souls are very angry, confused and scared for various reasons. One such entity was in a house in Hotchkiss, not too far from where I lived. It was really wreaking havoc on the family, banging on walls, slamming doors, and raising hell in general. When I received a call for help, I asked my friend, Polly, to come and assist me.

Upon entering the house, we could feel the presence of more than one. The first one left without resistance. The second was not at all willing to leave; it was having too much fun scaring the daylights out of the family.

I felt that the lady of the house, who had put out the call for help, was at a very low vibration, thus in some way holding onto the bodiless entity. So, I began cleaning her up by raising her vibration to an acceptable level in order to release it. In the meantime, Polly was doing her work outside—opening up a portal for those who wished to leave.

I called on my buddy, Archangel Michael, and using a very powerful crystal, finally got the entity to leave. I did have to chase after him into the master bedroom and finally into the bathroom, where he was hiding. Then, finally, he left, and as far as I know, never returned. The last time I checked, all was quiet and serene at the home.

A Bigfoot Encounter:

There is a mystical place known as Idyllwild. It rests at the foot of a towering granite mountain. Many come there, not quite understanding why. All they know is that it feels so very special. This is due to the high energy of the area.

I had the privilege of residing there for a short time and its energy seemed to bring out the child in me. It really got my creative juices flowing—the music for my children's story, "Song of the Golden Eagle," was pouring out of me.

One day, while exploring a wooded area, I came upon a mountain stream gushing around the foot of this towering granite rock. Following for a ways I suddenly felt as though I was no longer alone. Someone or something was watching me. Turning around I tried peering through the trees. Nothing unusual caught my eye. However, there still was that feeling of being watched.

I didn't feel any fear, just a sort of a curiosity and a high burst of excitement. It was something akin to the energy I had felt when I sighted Bashar's space ship, but lacking the high vibration of love.

I remember asking out loud, "Who are you?" Everything seemed to have become so very silent, even the birds had hushed their song.

The only audible sound was the gurgling of the mountain stream, rushing to wherever it was headed.

"Must have been my imagination," I thought, making my way back toward my car. However, for some reason, I decided to take a different route and not follow the stream. Instead, I chose to climb up to where a large, rather flat rock was and proceed down from there.

Just prior to parking my car, there had been a nice cooling shower, which left the ground soggy and damp. Climbing up to the rock, my eyes widened in amazement. There, embedded next to it in the wet ground, was a giant footprint. It wasn't human, but similar, and it definitely wasn't animal, or at least none that I was familiar with.

Was it possible that it could belong to a Bigfoot? If so, what on earth was it doing here? I was so excited, I ran to my car, jumped in, and speeded back to get my friends with whom I was staying. They just had to see this.

Breathlessly I told them what I had found. Immediately they swung into action, gathered some materials they had stored in their home, and back we went to make a cast of the large footprint.

Upon arriving back at the rock, they inspected the print. "Could it be a bear?" I queried.

"If it is, then it's a different kind than has ever been around here," Lee quickly answered. They were as excited as I, and quickly mixed up the material to make the cast.

While waiting for it to harden, I told them about my experience of feeling I wasn't alone and the silence that had prevailed around me. We speculated that if it was a Bigfoot, he must have been on that flat rock. Then when I started coming toward it, jumped down, running into the thick forest. The print must have been made when he landed. We searched for more prints. We thought we saw a part of one, but weren't certain.

Finally the cast had hardened. Carefully picking it up, they placed it on a large flat board they had brought with them, and back to the house we went.

The next morning Lee got a call from a neighbor who lived a small distance from the town. "You're not going to believe this," Lee told him. Then, after telling him, said, "Why don't you come and see what you make of it?"

He dashed over, and after viewing our find said, "Now it's your turn. Come over to my place and take a look at what's in my back yard."

He said that he had been visited by a Bigfoot and a couple of small "children," and that he had been able to communicate telepathically with them.

Sure enough, in their back yard, which was a part of a mountain rising above them, were quite a few prints, somewhat faded. However they did resemble the one that we had set in a cast along with smaller, similar ones.

From his description of that night, and his close encounter, it must have been quite a wild one. His wife said that she was really frightened. When her husband tried to get her to join him/them, she refused, staying inside the house.

I recalled Bashar telling us about Bigfoot. He said that they are sometimes dropped off in certain areas of Planet Earth by space ships, evidently for exploration. He also said that they had the ability to appear and disappear whenever the scenario called for it. That is why "now you see them, now you don't"—like space ships.

Eventually the print crumbled. My friends didn't have the one ingredient necessary to keep that from happening. If we had been lucky enough to have preserved it, then you might have been reading this in the newspaper.

However, all I can do is relate what the others and I experienced that late afternoon and night upon that mystical mountain with its gigantic granite rock rising to the sky.

These are but a sampling of what I have encountered while doing my work of Awakenings, et cetera. There are many parallel worlds and many other existences that we are not aware of, or won't let ourselves see due to the programming and teachings we have received. Unaware people beget unaware people until finally, somehow, someway we break through the mold and rise above those teachings, those beliefs.

What I have discovered is, that due to my willingness to break out of the mold, allowing myself to explore other worlds, other possibilities, I now know that other worlds and other beings, do exist—and not just within the confines of my mind. They are real and, when the timing is right and we are willing to experience them, they will appear. Believe me, I know that BELIEVING IS SEEING. If we wait to see before we believe, then we just might be waiting and waiting and waiting, while life and the exciting real world passes us by.

What you fear will appear

AND

What you resist will persist

THE DNA CAPER

(An unbelievable true story)

There are two kinds of power operating on Planet Earth at this time—that which we call negative or the Dark, and that which we call positive or the Light. They are also known as the polarities, and due to their differences create separation for us to explore and experience.

Their vibrations are worlds apart. One is vibrating at a very high ratio, thus creating a lighter, more transparent appearance, while the other is vibrating at a very low ratio, thus creating a dense or solid appearance. And, of course, there are all shades in between.

When we place our attention on either of them, we then feed it our power, thus enhancing its power. So it stands to reason that if we fear something negative is going to happen, and continue focusing and worrying about it, we begin creating the exact thing we don't want to happen. This is how we manifest the negative, *for what we fear will appear.*

However, by letting go of our negative thoughts and re-creating the scenario in a positive way, with love, we then are no longer lending our power to that which we do not wish to happen. Thus we reinforce the positive while eliminating the negative.

Worrying that something is going to happen is one of the best ways to feed that negative scenario and bring it about. Fear and worry go hand in hand as does love and trust. So, since there are these two polarities operating within our reality, let us look at both of them with discernment in order to be able to choose which one we would rather be supporting.

Since it matters not what names or labels we place upon them, let us call the lower vibration the Dark, because of its density, and the higher vibration the Light, due to its lightness—the higher the vibration, the lighter the density.

One is cunning, devious, using lies and trickery, unrelenting in its endeavor *to win at* all cost. The other is, at times, very gullible, believing all is light and goodness, and because they are of the Light how can anything but good happen to them? They are also very reluctant to use force in order to protect themselves.

However, sometimes the use of force is necessary. Probably even more important is that we need to throw some Light into the Dark so they, too, can learn. After all, the Dark also needs lessons, how else are they to see "the error of their ways" and become Light?

If we, the Light, feel that we are losing the battle, perhaps we had better take another look at our responsibility in this scenario, namely being responsible for self. There have been many incidents of giving our power away by not being discerning and taking the necessary action to protect our selves. We then allow the Dark to be the "conqueror" and we the so-called "victim." The bottom line is always for experience.

Perhaps we did need the lesson, the experience. However, the time has come to not be so trusting, and to take a stand against anyone who is trying to take our power, even if they try to tell us that it is for our own good. We've had our lessons, and now it is time for us to teach through our actions.

There have been many instances of us being too gullible, of believing

56

and trusting those who may not have been very trustworthy. They may appear to be walking in the Light, thus throwing us off guard. However, it behooves us all to be more discerning, to question intentions and motives before we go handing our power over to anybody. In fact, we should never hand our power to anyone. Those of the Light would never even suggest such a thing.

A wonderful example of those feeding the Dark, yet believing that they are serving the Light was written several years ago. This article referred to them as the Twilight People. Their vibration is not of the Light, but they are always walking in the facade of being the Light, thus tricking those who are walking their path in trust. They usually aren't even aware of what they are doing.

You may not recognize them at first. However, soon after having been in their energy for a while, you will find your own vibration taking a nose-dive. Outward appearance can be very deceiving. That is, until we learn to "pay attention" to our Inner Voice.

This has happened to me more than once, and before I knew it, I was sucked into their "loving" vibration. This is not an uncommon occurrence, but eventually we do learn to be more discerning.

One of the scenarios of giving our power away, which had happened in the far distant past, was shown to me in vivid detail and, as they say, in "Glorious Technicolor." I will never forget that day nor that experience. It all began when I decided to take a drive up into the mountains.

It was a beautiful summer day in late August. I had gone up to a lovely little restaurant for breakfast, where the mountains rise majestically, creating a scenic background for the little resort. I had just finished eating and, while lingering over another cup of coffee, was reading the book, *Bringers of the Dawn,* channeled to Barbara Marciniak by the Pleiadians.

As I began reading another chapter, I felt a sort of nudge, like something was trying to open me up to another awareness, but that soon passed, so I continued reading. This chapter was giving information of how ten strands of our DNA were removed from our reality, leaving us with only two, thus diminishing our power ten-twelfths or more.

"Come on," I said to myself in disbelief, for it certainly was unreal to me at that time. "What kind of BS is this?" Evidently there were others tuned into what I was thinking, for suddenly I started feeling very light-headed, unbalanced and a bit emotional.

My answer was "pay your bill and leave the restaurant." This seemed the best thing to do, for, from past experience, I have learned that it is best to act immediately when my guides give such a direct order.

So, paying my bill and grabbing my book and keys, I started driving. I remember thinking/asking, "This is about the DNA, isn't it?" The answer was clear and precise. "Yes!" Thus I embarked upon a journey into the distant past, which lasted close to five hours and opened up a dark and painful time. It also gave me a new insight into why I have behaved and acted—reacted is a better word—to life the way I have.

They then directed me to get back on the highway that had a wonderful scenic view. Driving around the dam, I could feel myself becoming more and more emotional. I hadn't the foggiest of where "they," whom I presumed were my guides, were taking me, but feeling compelled to drive, did so. Someone or something was pulling the strings and it wasn't me.

Not wanting to get into some kind of an uncontrollable situation on a main highway, which I felt was inevitable, I looked for a turnoff, some place to stop or at least a less traveled road. About six miles before reaching the top of the pass, They said, "Turn here!" This I did, turning off onto a dirt road.

Driving only a short distance on that road, all hell broke loose. It was as though I were in another time and space. I could feel myself being held down by some kind of tractor beam. I remember screaming, yelling, pleading. "Please, please, don't do this to me."

Feeling sick, I stopped and got out of the car. This helped to ground me a little, but I was still pretty much out of it. It was like a nightmare that I couldn't quite awaken from.

Finally, getting back into my car, I drove higher up the mountain. Parking my car, I started walking down a trail that stopped at the edge of a cliff. Below me stretched a peaceful little valley surrounded by aspen and tall pine trees. Leaning against a large brother pine, a wave of terror seized me. My body was shaking. Once again I was pulled back into that horrible nightmare of reliving the past, forced to face its painful memories.

It was as though my power was being drained from me and my knowingness shut down until I was only a minuscule part of who I had been. There was no compassion, no love. I felt like an animal being dissected by scientists, completely helpless and at their mercy, which was zilch. Hatred, anger, hopelessness was rising within me as this continued.

You S.O.B.s, you DBs, you #?!$&*^!"*#$!#"*, you, you," I could hear myself yelling words which would never be acceptable in polite society.

I can't remember ever having felt such tremendous hatred and hopelessness as I did during the reliving of this ordeal. The last thing I remember of this scenario was something being superimposed upon one of my two remaining strands of DNA.

On one had been written fear, hate, judgment, and all of those negative emotions, while the other was left with my original unconditional love. Try balancing those two, lifetime after lifetime, which evidently I have been trying to do ever since.

Suddenly the vision of reliving that ancient time lifted. Once again I was sitting on the ground with my back against a tree. Believe me, I was really happy to be back in present time. The peaceful little valley was a welcome sight. There seemed also to be a feeling of peace rising within, along with a new awareness of how the past has affected my present and other lifetimes.

One thing this reliving of that past experience has done for me is to give me the awareness of the reasons behind the no-win, love-hate game that has been so prevalent on this planet for so long.

It also answered my ever-burning question, "Why couldn't I love or allow myself to receive love?" And why was the longing for love so strong? Of course, this all went hand in hand with not loving myself and always setting myself up for failure, whether it was relationships or whatever.

The Pleiadians really did create quite an interesting experimental station here on Planet Earth. They even admit to that in their newer book, Earth. We were their laboratory animals to be experimented on in whatever way they decided. The experiments are still going on today.

However, this time it is our governments being the so-called "bad guys," not the Pleiadians.

They, the Pleiadians, are now coming down to right the wrong and to work with us in our mission to assist Mother Earth and her children. Evidently, they can't advance any further until we do—another Cosmic Joke. It is, however, all a part of the Divine Plan, which is becoming clearer as we evolve into higher states of awareness.

How did so many of us get caught in this predicament? Well, we were a trusting lot, and we did volunteer to experience the negative side. I believe you will agree with me that it would be hard to create a better win-lose game than the love vs. hate one. It can really create a raging battle within.

How can we rise above this no-win game? The only way out, as far as I know, is love. As Mother Meera says, *Love is the ultimate tool or weapon to change or combat anything that is blocking your path to the light. For pure love can never be defeated. It is infinite.* And She is only one of many Masters whose message is Love. In fact, Love is the only true message.

I know that Unconditional Love is the highest vibration that can be attained. Since keeping our vibration high is imperative in order to free ourselves, then why judge whatever happened in the past? Judgment sticks you to the incident you are judging and is, in itself, a trap. Besides, *you cannot judge and love at the same time—it is impossible.*

Since it is very important to keep our vibration as high as possible in order to stay clear of negativity, it behooves all of us to love ourselves and everything else, unconditionally, and let go of our judgments.

How do we let go of judgment? By always being in the moment. It isn't hard when you love each moment, whatever it may be, without judging it. Look upon everything as an experience—a lesson to assist you in evolving, and be thankful for that lesson. Whatever happened yesterday, or five minutes ago, you created or co-created with the help of others—so take responsibility for it and move on.

Always being thankful will eliminate any judgments. Learn to discern and see the real reason for having created or co-created the scenario.

When one "gets the lesson," there is always a jump in awareness.

Thank yourself, the scenario and all who participated and, if there is any residue of judgments, release them immediately. Otherwise you may find yourself back in the same old "habitual ritual" soup again.

I did, many times, until I became thankful instead of judging whatever I was experiencing. Thus I no longer create unwanted scenarios.

I will agree that it is very difficult to love a scenario, which is so traumatic that it feels like it is tearing your very life apart. However, once we stop resisting and relax into it, the lesson or awareness of why we put ourselves into that situation will appear. Then whatever judgment we have placed upon that scenario can be removed, allowing us to savor the sweet essence of our new awareness and the power we have gained by going through it.

The reason why I allowed this to occur was revealed to me much later. I now know that it was a part of my chosen path, which is giving me a more expanded and meaningful view of my journey here on Planet Earth.

Now, instead of judging, I thank those who participated as well as myself for the scenario. This then enables me to move on to a more exciting and ever-expanding awareness.

Why carry around a big bag full of judgments, and grudges? All they will do is make one stoop-shouldered and old. Is it really worth it? Only you can answer that question.

The game of life is

ever expanding, ever changing
as we evolve
into
higher realms of
consciousness

ARCHANGEL MICHAEL AND HIS

GOLDEN EAGLES OF LIGHT

Archangel Michael gave this message to me. It was more like a command than a message and started out very abruptly:

My Golden Eagles are scattered, their light has been dimmed. They are floundering, unable to rise above the murky illusion of Planet Earth. Their light is needed to complete the Divine Plan of the Great and Glorious Creator. Find and Awaken them. Bring them out of their state of forgetfulness so that they may once again join me. IT IS TIME!

This was the same kind of energy I felt a few years earlier when I was visiting my son, Jimmy, in Taos, New Mexico. I had gone up to do some Awakenings and was busy cleansing my crystals, not into meditation or anything, just feeling happy and alive. No one was in the room with me.

Suddenly this message came through. It was very powerful, almost bowling me over. I remember crying from its impact.

The message was:

"THE DARK FORCES ARE GATHERING FOR THEIR FINAL ATTACK AGAINST THE LIGHT—MAKE READY!" It ended as abruptly as it started.

My body was trembling, for I wasn't quite ready for that high of an energy—being new at this game of the Awakenings at that time. Nor did I have the slightest idea who or what was giving me the message.

It wasn't until much later that I became aware that this powerful energy I have come to know and love was Archangel Michael. All I knew was I had been given a message, and really didn't have the slightest idea what to do with it. Of course, now I am very aware of why that message was given to me as well as to many others.

Who are the Golden Eagles? Well, the best way I can explain them is to relate this story as Archangel Michael told it to me. If it rings a bell or you feel a nudge, like a door to your memory trying to open, then you probably are one. If not, it still will make for an interesting piece of reading. However, don't discount the validity of it too quickly.

This is the story as told to me by Archangel Michael:

A long time ago there was what is referred to as a War in the Heavens. The Great Creator had, in Its infinite wisdom, created two very powerful energies—Love and Fear. The reason for this was for choice, so Free Will could make Its own decision as to what It wanted to be and do—for if there were nothing to choose from, then what would be the reason to have Free Will?

Love was and still is the highest energy that can be obtained. So, because of this awesome power, Fear chose to go the opposite direction in order to be as powerful, or even greater. Thus Ego came into existence, causing separation through judgment, but in the eyes of The Creator all is equal.

Love had all the properties of the higher vibrations—i.e., beauty, joy, wealth, health, understanding and compassion—in great abundance.

The other vibration of Fear, along with Ego and Judgment, created the so-called negative energies of hate, greed, control, pain, suffering, lack of, et cetera, also in great abundance. So now there were two very powerful forces working against each other, which was creating quite a commotion within what was, until then, a tranquil and peaceful existence.

Since it was not possible for both, a traumatic and a peaceful state, to reside within the same area, The Great Creator felt it best that one leave and reside elsewhere.

Sides were chosen by the individual energies residing therein. Archangel Michael, representing Love, called His Golden Eagles of Light to his side, while the Angel Beelzebub, who has carried the name of Satan/Lucifer, called upon those who felt drawn to experience the negative or so-called dark polarity.

A great battle ensued, the outcome of which was that Angel Beelzebub and his followers were expelled from what is referred to as Heaven, and love and tranquillity reigned once again.

Planet Earth became the fertile ground where both polarities have established residence. The battle between "good and evil" has been and still is being fought to this day."

I then asked, "But aren't we all one?"

Yes, in a sense. However, when we separated from The One, we each took on an individual vibration, which is referred to as our Signature Vibration, thus vibrating at different frequencies. The purpose being to make each Spirit more individualized, more recognizable to self as well as to each other.

So, this was the beginning of the separation and also the beginning of creating universes, including rocks and other inanimate beings. However, each and everything is the reflection of The Great I AM, THE ALL THAT IS, experiencing Itself in every conceivable and non-conceivable way. Do you understand?

"Yes, thank you."

"Good! I now am going to expound upon the so-called war in heaven.' The channel that is known to you as Penny (Penelope A. Greenwell) mentioned this in her communication to you. She said that Lucifer, who was known as The Morning Star, really has gotten a bad rap on Planet Earth. She is in the progress of writing her own story regarding this, which will bring to light the truth.*

"Lucifer and I were together during the oneness of all. You could refer

to us as twin souls, which we all were until we were split apart at the time of the separation.

"I chose one path, he chose the other. However, we both were in the service of The Great I AM, fulfilling our chosen roles. Of course, we were not the only ones, so where there was once one, now there were many, each with the purpose of serving The Great I AM in two distinctly different ways, i.e., the way of the Light and the way of the Dark of the Light.

This left each soul with a deep longing to be reunited with the other. Also, there was a feeling of abandonment as well as loneliness. However, each had chosen their path and now was committed to the task of carrying it out to the end.

Thus the Dark of the Light is attracted to the Light, and, of course, the Light is attracted to the Dark. And so the great conflict to remain whichever each chose to be has created the feeling of imbalance, of not being complete. It also has left the feeling of not quite being certain who each is.

The Great I AM is experiencing itself in both polarities, with no judgment, only Unconditional Love.

This struggle, this game will be ended when each individual understands him/her self completely and realizes they no longer desire to be a part of this game—this illusion. They then will integrate themselves, allowing the Dark of the Light to become Light or Enlightened.

As this occurs, the more expanded Soul-Self will also be raised higher in awareness, for there is never an end to achieving awareness. The creation of THE ALL THAT IS extends throughout Infinity.

When all have come to that point of complete integration, the slate will be wiped clean. No score is kept, for there are neither winners nor losers.

The game we call life is ever expanding, ever evolving, ever exploring. The Great I AM is constantly creating, erasing, reforming, becoming more of Itself within THE ALL THAT IS.

Clouds are a perfect reflection of this phenomenon. Watch them. You can learn a lot about life from clouds.

I leave you within the love and light of The Great I AM.

I AM ARCHANGEL MICHAEL.

That was the end of my lesson, which left me with much to chew on and digest.

From time to time Archangel Michael has sent his Golden Eagles down to assist those who wish to turn back to the Light. However, because the Illusion, a/k/a the Veil of Forgetfulness, exists here on Planet Earth, many have been caught in its web and are unable to remember why they are here or who they are. Thus the call from Archangel Michael—IT IS TIME. FIND AND AWAKEN THEM!

At this time—the beginning of a new era—there are many Golden Eagles of Light here to assist us with this mission. Once in a while, especially if you are a Golden Eagle, you will feel someone's vibration so strong, so powerful that you will be drawn to it like a magnet and they to you.

This will especially be true when they are vibrating in their light—the power of their truth. For some are vibrating at such a high intensity of love and compassion that you will want to bathe in that glow forever.

However, some are not in such a high state of vibration. They are the ones that Archangel Michael has charged us with the task of finding and awakening. They are still floundering within the Mass Consciousness and weighted down by its heavy vibration.

Their wings have been covered with Illusion's fears, anger, guilt, pain from the judgments they have heaped upon themselves as they struggle to find their path, to fulfill their commitment. They have forgotten who they are and why they are here. They feel that they are on Planet Earth for a specific reason, but can't remember what it is.

They also know, deep in their heart, that the so-called "truth" with which they have been bombarded by religions, governments, families, friends and leaders are lies or, at best, half-truths.

The illusion on Planet Earth has muffled their light, diminished their power and their awareness—thus shutting down their ability to receive true communication from their Higher Source.

Still they struggle onward, trying this, that and the other, always reaching for the key which will unlock the door to their dilemma and set them free.

They want to soar and sometimes they have vague recollections of being able to, but the heavy foot of Mass Consciousness comes down hard, blocking out those precious memories and the door to real freedom slams shut again.

Sometimes they will hear a voice or get a thought as though someone or some Higher Power is trying to get a message through to them—telling them not to give up, to keep on searching. This is what keeps them reaching for the Light, but they reach outside of self, turning to drugs and other outside influences.

This will, sooner or later, entrap them further within the illusion of forgetfulness. All they would have to do to free themselves is go within, for that is where their truth lies. It was placed there by The Creator so they would never become lost.

However, they have become lost, not to God but to themselves and their commitment. Why has this happened? I haven't been given the answer to that one, but I am certain that it has something to do with us coming down to experience, to learn.

This was to give us more power, more understanding in order to be of greater service to the Light. The Illusion did snare a bunch of us.

The plan was to experience and learn how to handle those negative energies. Once experiencing them, we then would have a much greater understanding and compassion for those who were trapped by the negative and were struggling to be free.

However, some of us did get caught up in Illusion's judgments. I have been aware of this for some time, for I, too, was deeply buried in that dark illusion. Yet I kept hearing a voice from somewhere telling me that there was more to life than struggle, failure, disappointment and death.

Sometimes I felt that I knew, but what was it I knew? I might get a glimpse of a knowingness beyond what I was told was the truth; then all would shut down again.

Of course, the DNA experience that I told about earlier played a big part in this phenomenon of getting me off my path and shutting me down, along with many others. After all, we were and still are a very powerful light to reckon with. And, as Archangel Michael says—it is time for us all to awaken!

So my light had been dimmed, my "wings" were nowhere to be found, and I definitely was not flying. I had been caught in the Mass Consciousness, where war, hate, greed, and control reigned supreme.

Talk about hell all you want, but there is no truer hell than what a

Golden Eagle experiences when he/she can no longer soar—when they have strayed off of their path and know that they have made a commitment but can't remember what it is.

This is when our Gold Ray can really explode us into situations we usually wouldn't even consider. We keep trying to break out of the cage we have let ourselves be put into, and only end up getting deeper into the mire through the misuse of our Gold Ray—i.e., using its awesome power negatively and then judging our actions.

I'm sure we have all been told at some time that we are afraid of our power, which is true. This stems from our misuse of it and the judgment we placed on it at that time, which is waiting to be brought to the surface and released.

Eventually, though, someone does recognize our light, our true vibration, and assists us in getting out of the trap and back on our path. When this happens, and we realize who we are and why we are here, that is when we really start "champing at the bit" to get back into the saddle and complete the mission we came here to do.

This happened for me in Santa Fe. I had just about given up and felt my life force was fading—that soon I would be leaving the planet—but that was not to be. For instead of my life coming to an end, as thought, it was only the beginning of what my real life was to be.

Awaken the Master

Within

It is time!

THE AWAKENINGS

Feel the power of God's love and light
Guiding you through your darkest fright
Then feel that power surging deep within
For when love is your power, the healing begins

There are many new and powerful energies coming onto the planet now to assist us in raising our vibration and expanding our awareness. All we have to do is be willing to respond by opening up to those energies that call to us.

I was ready to leave California, and since I didn't know where I really wanted to go, headed for Taos, New Mexico. My son, Jimmy, had come to California earlier and, at my request, had taken my Doberman/Rottweiler, Thor, back to Taos.

Thor had outgrown his cute little puppy stage and needed someone to assist him in making the transition into becoming a responsible adult. So Jimmy took him to Taos and turned him into a wonderful, obedient, personal guard dog. It seems as though Thor was always pulling us together.

Anyway, I landed in Taos, which Jimmy loved and I tolerated. I just couldn't seem to get into its vibration. The right vibration is so very necessary for each of us—the vibration of where we live, those we are with. The list goes on and on, for everything is vibration, and the more compatible the vibration, the more joyous our life becomes.

Most important of all is to find that vibration which is the closest to our own Signature Vibration—the true vibration of who we are. When all of our bodies—physical, emotional, mental and spiritual—are vibrating together in this natural rhythm, then we truly are in our joy.

However, since the physical body is more dense, be patient and treat it with the love and respect it deserves. After all, it has been a wonderful home for us while spending time on Planet Earth.

The channelings of Bashar had opened my awareness to a great extent. However, my physical body seemed to be going the other direction. I had no energy, thus it was hard to make myself do anything. My enthusiasm for life had all but disappeared.

To make matters worse, I discovered that the house we had rented up on Pot Creek above Taos had radon gas, which was poisoning us. Jimmy was really being affected by it. He was as pale as a ghost and I could hardly walk, so we decided to move. He went over to another little mountain town, and I went to Santa Fe.

Taking up residence in a small apartment connected to a larger house that a friend was renting, I had a feeling that I wasn't long for this world. My life force seemed to be deteriorating to the point where everything was an effort. That was when The Awakenings first came into my life.

A friend told me about Jim Raintree and Helen Reid. They had come into Santa Fe to give Awakenings and magical things were happening to those who received one.

Now I had tried many things over this lifetime, some of which had given me a "quickie fix" with no permanent or lasting result. Nevertheless, at my friend's insistence, which was nothing compared to my guides' steady bombardment, I decided to check it out, so made an appointment.

Upon arriving at the motel where the Awakenings were taking place, I was greeted by a small, vivacious blonde lady, who laughingly said she was Ralph. This, I found out, was her counterpart. She then introduced me to Jim Raintree, who is a descendant of the Mayan Indians. His counterpart's name was "Peggy Sue."

I was almost blown over by such a high vibration of love and light. It was such a pleasure just being around them. Their mission was to bring in the love and the light, thus restoring our childlike giggle of happiness, which most of us have lost along the way.

I must admit, they were really masters of this. Whenever I was with them, I found myself joyfully laughing from their high humor and energy—they were like a breath of fresh air.

It was time for my first Awakening, which was nothing like anything I had ever experienced before. It was, as they had said, a dance between my Higher Whole Soul Self and me, along with the Masters, Angels, Guides, all congregating in that one room, guiding and orchestrating the dance—and what a dance!

To say the least, it was beautiful, uplifting, and awesome. It opened up locked doors, releasing negative energies, such as judgment, anger and self-blame, replacing those damaging thoughts with light and love for myself—the missing ingredient I had for so long searched.

Since I had piled so much of Illusion's negative "stuff" on me with judgments of myself, and also buying the judgment of others, it didn't happen all at once. After all, it had taken me many moons to dig the hole as deeply as I had dug mine.

However, I knew this time I had found the way out. Can you imagine the joyful feeling I was experiencing—not only knowing that there was a way out, but to actually find the path which would lead me there, giving me some purpose for living? At long last there was a light at the end of the tunnel, and it was brightly shining, calling to me.

Of course, it's shining for everyone. All one has to do is find their true path and follow it. Once that happens, everything becomes crystal clear, giving purpose and fulfillment to one's life.

With each Awakening, more and more negativity will rise up and be released. The magical thing is that, if allowed, the experience on the table continues long after the actual Awakening has ended. However, one must be willing for that to happen, and not shut themselves down with their fears and judgments.

After my first Awakening, I laid in my little apartment for three days, crying, laughing, and detoxifying, which brought me to higher and higher knowingness. I did get up and meet them for breakfast each morning. It was such a pleasure being around their high energy. My world was changing fast, giving it a new and meaningful outlook.

On the third day after my Awakening, they informed me that they were leaving for Arizona the next morning. It was as though I were being guided by an unseen hand, for I packed some clothes, climbed into my little car, and went with them to Tucson—their first stop. Having lived in Phoenix, I wanted to get them with as many of my friends as I could. In fact, I wanted everyone to meet them and experience an Awakening.

After Tucson and Phoenix, we traveled to Los Angeles. I stayed with a friend and they took a motel on the beach, where they continued doing their work. After completing their mission in the Los Angeles area, we then went to the little mountain town of Idyllwild. This is where I was privileged to witness another miracle.

A friend of mine brought his ex-wife up to them in a wheelchair. She was unable to walk, due to some kind of a degenerating disease. However, after The Awakening, she walked out—a little shaky, but walking.

Did she maintain her newfound ability? This I do not know, for I never heard. We each choose what we wish to experience for our growth. However, I do know that she had been shown that she could walk, and the rest was up to her.

So, as I said, my world was changing, and fast. Along with the change came more awareness, more love for myself and for everything else that I could feel, see and touch. I was also experiencing more body energy—my life force was back—big time.

After saying goodbye to Ralph and Peggy Sue, I headed back to Santa Fe and they to their home in Florida. Shortly after arriving home,

I received a letter saying that they were going to give an Intensive in the fall, which would enable those who attended to do The Awakenings. Would I like to join them? It didn't take me any longer than a New York second to decide.

I didn't have a clue as to how I was to come up with the money for the trip and to pay for the Intensive. However, Spirit does work in wondrous ways and, in a few days, I sold a piece of property that I had been trying to sell for years, bought my ticket, and was on my way to Florida and the Intensive, along with some of my friends from Santa Fe.

Jim and Helen met us at the airport—what a happy reunion that was. They then drove us to a beautiful white sandy beach, where there was only one large house in sight. It had floor-to-ceiling windows exposing a breathtaking scene of blue water, sunshine and that white sandy beach. This was to be our home for 10 days, where magical things were to happen.

There were fourteen of us locked together in that high energy of Love and Light. This is where a group, working together in complete harmony of purpose, can be so very powerful. During those ten days, we learned how to call in The Masters of Light/Angels of Love, releasing the dark, negative energies through their guidance.

Once having experienced that phenomenon, you then will know when that energy is there, and when it isn't. If that high energy is not called in and is not present to guide and oversee the Awakening, then it isn't much of a "party." In other words, there is only Ego directing, which adds up to an empty ritual with very little or no effect. I kid you not, once experiencing the energy of the Masters/Angels, you will know.

During that time, we were so "in synch" with each other that it did not matter where any of us were—walking the beach, swimming or whatever—we could feel the energies starting to build and we all knew that it was time to return for another Awakening session.

Dolphins would come and be as close to the shoreline as they could get. On our last day, before leaving to go back home, a mother dolphin and her baby were seen leaping out of the water. As I said before, it was a magical time.

There have been many openings of awareness achieved through The Awakenings. My first Awakening was awesome. However, with each one more and more understanding of myself, and my many and varied actions/reactions came to light.

No two Awakenings are alike. Once a layer of "stuff" has been released, then another layer rises to the surface for releasing, and so on, until we hit the very core, which is the crux of our negativity.

Once we rise out from under all of our "stuff," we then are able to see the truth of who we really are. This is when we begin loving ourselves, unconditionally. For when we see the glorious Beings we are, what is there for us not to love? We truly are the reflection of God in all of Its magnificence.

Some of our Space Brothers refer to us as "the shell people," because of the layers of "stuff" we have piled upon ourselves, dimming our true light. When all of the layers have been removed, we then can be masters of our own destiny.

Since we all have enlisted others along the way to assist in co-creating this game we call life, they, too, will appear from time to time in whatever scenario we are exploring during an Awakening

Sometimes it will be the ones we feel closest to. Some may be those whom we have termed "mortal enemies," but when the scenario is revisited, then understanding and love replaces blame and judgment, thus another layer is removed.

Many times our Animal Guides, as well as Gurus and Masters, appear. There has been many Awakening when the Awakenee became acquainted with one or more of their Animal Guides for the first time. One lady came out of the Awakening room in amazement at seeing a beautiful huge buffalo. She had never been aware of such a thing as Animal Guides until then. She is now, and is closely connected to it.

Of course, Angels, our Higher Self and our own special Guardian Angels are always with us and have been since the beginning, even though we may not be aware of them on this level. Then, upon touching in on them in an Awakening, they become very real and accessible to the individual.

With the Intensive over, I went back home. My energy was zooming and I was really coming out of my long sleep of forgetfulness. I was beginning to remember, to be tuned in to what was, for me, "the real life."

I could hardly wait to get started on awakening others to their truth—to begin fulfilling the commitment I had made so long ago. As Archangel Michael said, "IT IS TIME."

Experiencing an Awakening:

Upon arriving home, I began gathering the tools which I will need to do Awakenings—a folding massage table, my special family of crystals, candles, incense, music to play, which is conducive to releasing negative energies.

I am always told what music to play. If I get into my head and believe something else would be better, I find that either the tape won't play or that which "I" have chosen is not the right energy needed for that Awakening. I then find myself having to change back to the one suggested.

One does learn to pay attention and to get out of trying to control when the Masters, Higher Self, Angels and Guides are around. They don't put up with any Ego nonsense—not for a minute.

So the scene is set. The candles are lit. The counseling has taken place, pin-pointing the exact problems, and the Awakeners have gathered around the Awakening table. Crystals have been washed and cleansed, and the one receiving the Awakening is lying on the table, as a prayer is offered, invoking God to bring forth the protection of Light and Love. The Masters, Higher Soul Self and Angels are always invited, for within them lies the Power of The Awakenings.

Many wonderful things happen during an Awakening. Some of which I will try to bring forth in order to give you a better understanding of how I raised my vibration to higher awareness.

As the music plays—and it always seems to be perfect for whatever is needed for that particular Awakening—negative energies begin to rise to the surface. First to come off will be the ones which are more within the awareness, such as anger, grief, blame. Negative thoughts that no longer are of service will also appear to be released to the Light. And, when appropriate, a journey back to past lifetimes is taken, where trauma and judgment has played havoc with the present lifetime, creating physical, emotional and mental turmoil.

All of this, however, can only be accomplished at the discretion of the Higher Self, who always has the final say—only the Higher Self knows what is to be released at any given time for the individual's highest good. In other words, it definitely is a dance between you and your Higher Self.

So, now having set the scene, here are some of the things that I have experienced both in receiving and also giving Awakenings.

The prayer has been offered, calling in the protection of the Light. Music is playing, and my eyes are closed, which the awakenee is always asked to do. Suddenly, I feel more than see whom I believe to be my soul mate, my Golden Eagle. His mighty wings carry me upward as I am held safe in his strong arms.

We go past a beautiful crystal city, soaring ever higher. I can feel his love for me and mine for him, and the feeling is so intense, so beautiful, that I never want to return. Being united with my love, from whom so long separated now by the veil, I knew we were and always would be together. Thus I was given the encouragement I needed to continue raising my vibration until no longer would that veil separate us.

Just before returning to Earth's plane, a beautiful rose that looked as if it had been dipped in gold was presented to me. Then Lord Jesus appeared, carrying a large ruby heart—a symbol of His Unconditional Love for all of us.

As I was returning to my body, I heard Jim, the lead Awakener, ask, "Did you guys see that huge golden eagle carry her away—and Lord Jesus with that ruby heart?" Evidently he was really tuned into my Awakening and me.

Oh yes, one more thing that happened in this Awakening. My son, Jimmy, who had committed suicide a couple of years earlier, and his cousin, Tad, who had made his exit from Planet Earth with an overdose of drugs, appeared right at the beginning, before Golden Eagle appeared—while the prayer was being offered. The odd part was that I hadn't been thinking about either of them, I was too engrossed in the prayer.

However, I saw and heard both very plainly—they seemed to have appeared out of nowhere and were talking to each other as they watched.

I heard Jimmy say, "This sure beats shooting up, doesn't it, Bro?" Tad then answered, "It sure does." This sounded so much like the way Jimmy would talk, if he were here on Earth, I started laughing, almost interrupting the prayer.

It is my reality that as we break through the barriers of Mass Consciousness, those who no longer are physically within our awareness can and will appear. Thus we are able to experience other worlds, other realities, which we probably never dreamed existed before breaking through that barrier.

Some of my Awakenings were very traumatic, bringing up old judgments, fears and blame. I remember sobbing my heart out on the table more than once from past incidents, some of which I had endured or had caused others to, and, of course, judged.

However, once the judgments are confronted and released, then the turmoil within subsides, leaving us peaceful, calm and loving. It's like all of those heavy burdens and judgments that we have carried around for so long have been removed and are no longer weighting us down. What a wonderful feeling of freedom that is.

It can also reverse the aging process, for once those heavy burdens of judgment and guilt have been removed and replaced with love, then there is a new spring to the step and a sparkle in the eye. The name of the game is to raise one's vibration and to change one's point of view, especially how one perceives oneself. This is easy, once our self-incriminating judgments no longer are bugging us.

One rather amusing incident happened when I was new at giving Awakenings. I was really releasing a lot of negative energy from the person I was working on. Suddenly I got this thought, "What happens to all of this negative stuff that we release?" I just didn't want to send it flying off into the universe, settling on others.

Then I was shown this picture. There were several rather small Light Beings with little golden buckets, standing back, away from the table. Every time a negative energy was released, they would catch it in their little buckets and turn it to light. They were so cute that I couldn't help but chuckle at the analogy I was being shown. It also told me that my concerns regarding those negative energies were groundless, and that we are always "in good hands."

I now tell others, as well as myself, when unwanted, negative thoughts come my way, *"put them in The Golden Bucket."* Or, as we have been told time and time again, "Let go and let God!" For some reason, visualizing all that stuff going into The Bucket and turning to Light really works for me. Try it—it just might do the same for you.

There have been several Awakenings, that I have given, which were, in themselves, awesome. One happened in Albuquerque, New Mexico. A friend and I were in the process of giving one to a lady who had just gotten out of prison. She had, in the past, been on drugs. Just as I finished the prayer, sensing something, I looked across the room and saw not one, but two, very ugly and frightening entities.

I never will forget them. The first one I saw was rather a light pea green with very little energy or intent. However, just behind it was the second one, which really got my attention. It was very dark, with fiery red eyes, some sort of a tail, and seemed very determined to not relinquish its hold upon the woman.

I took a couple of steps backward, as did my assistant. It was probably the ugliest creature I have ever encountered. I usually don't back down, but I must admit that I felt like turning tail and running. However, instead, I picked up a large generator crystal, which carries great energy, and went to work. Pointing the crystal directly toward them, I commanded them to leave.

The green one left—just dissolved into nothingness. The second one did just the opposite and seemed to become more powerful, bigger and, if possible, more ugly. I then called upon the powerful Angels of Light and felt their energy coming in.

Upon feeling their powerful and loving energy all around me, I knew that we now were protected, and so once again commanded that entity to release its hold on the lady. The dark entity became a blob of darkness and then disappeared altogether. She had probably collected that entity while either in prison or on drugs. That is when one is most susceptible to those low vibrational entities.

That handled, we continued with the Awakening, ending with the woman in a much higher vibration, laughing and happy. The heaviness appeared to have been removed. However, it wasn't over yet. It was getting almost dusk. Then, just before the lady left to go home, my very perceptive assistant suggested we follow her home. She felt that the entity might be somewhere around, just waiting for the chance to attach itself to the lady again.

So, following her home, sure enough, there was that dark but somehow not-so-powerful or scary entity lurking just outside her door. Again, calling upon the Angels, we commanded it to leave. It did, never to return—at least to our knowledge. Of course, these entities can be recreated again, if the person wants to have them around—their choice, always.

Another very memorable but different one was when a lady came to me for an Awakening. She had been gang-raped several times and, upon reliving that scenario, began throwing up. After releasing her from the rape incident, I noticed that the energy of a large cross was attached to her back across the shoulders. So I proceeded to release that energy.

The cross would get a few feet away, then back it would come. I then would release it and watch it go a few feet, then back it would come again. Finally, after several attempts, I decided that perhaps she wanted to keep it. Upon asking, she said no, she didn't. So, telling her to let it go, together we sent it on its way. This time it didn't return.

Many times we are not aware of just how or why we keep hanging onto things that no longer serve us. Sometimes we recreate the same thing over and over again—almost like a "habitual-ritual." Evidently we are so used to having them around, we feel unnatural without them.

I always invite those whom I consider the Highest of the High during the prayer to guide and direct me—Lord Jesus, Archangel Michael and His "Golden Eagles," The Council of Twelve, The Angels of Light, Mother Meera, Mother Mary, MeAmba and, of course, always Mother/Father God, as well as The Higher Soul Self, Guides, and Angels of the one receiving the Awakening. I would never think of doing an Awakening without them, for as I stated earlier, it wouldn't be much of an Awakening if they weren't there. It takes this kind of power, working as One, to accomplish that which I have witnessed in giving and receiving Awakenings.

Another unforgettable time for me was when I was doing an Awakening in Paonia. This girl was really into dramatizing her stuff—

big time. She must have really been enjoying her dramatization, for she was hanging onto it as though it were some kind of a prize possession, refusing to let go, even though her Higher Self said that it was time. In the meantime, I, for some reason, was getting caught up in her dramatization and was beginning to take it on. She had either been smoking pot, or had been around someone who had, and I seemed to be getting the full benefit of it.

As I kept pulling it off of her, I felt myself getting sleepy, sort of numb. I couldn't think and became aware that I no longer was receiving guidance from anyone. It was as though I was becoming part of her scenario.

For some reason, I felt I needed another crystal, so went over to where they were. Looking at the picture of the laughing Jesus, I asked, "What are you laughing at?" Suddenly Lord Jesus was standing right beside me and in a very unsympathetic voice replied, "THE DRAMATIZATION—GET OUT OF IT!"

Realizing what was happening, I released myself from her dramatization and proceeded with the Awakening, which turned out to be a great one. Believe me, that really was a very memorable one, and a great lesson to never get caught up in dramatizations, even my own.

It is magical to do an Awakening and watch the miracles take place. I know when someone is about to let go of their "stuff," for I can feel their pain, tears, anger, or whatever is rising to the surface. This tells me where to go to pull off those energies. I may feel tears streaming down my own cheeks, or get a pain someplace in my body. Then I know that is the place within their body that needs attention.

There will also be an indication when that action is complete, for it will be like a wave of release sweeping over me. There is no mistaking when the Awakening is finished. For me, it is like a smile that turns into a big grin when it has been completed. There also is a feeling of withdrawing of the intense energies that were there during the Awakening.

Jimmy, my son, received several Awakenings from me. He would come to me for an Awakening with a body heavy from misuse. He had been hooked on drugs since age 14. However, he always honored the Awakenings by fasting and staying clean for a few days prior to and after coming to me. I never ceased to be amazed at the apparent change that took place during an Awakening.

As he lay there on the table, I would call in his and my special Masters and Angels, and begin the process of releasing those negative energies. His vibration would go so high at those times that I would marvel at the speed with which he responded. It always felt like I was working with a Master who had come down to experience Earth in all its negativity. Those who have worked with him have said the same thing.

One Awakening I did on him was up in Taos, New Mexico, on a New Year's Eve during a full moon. What a wonderful, uplifting experience that was. New Year's Day we went out for dinner, and I couldn't keep my eyes off of him. He was vibrating at such a high level that he was almost transparent. Others who knew him were also remarking about his appearance.

Some lady came over and said, "You look just like Jesus." Jimmy, who has always had a great sense of humor, thoughtfully stroked his long reddish-brown beard for a moment and then replied, "Yes, I have been told that my Son resembles me." She got a startled look on her face for a moment, and then we both doubled over with laughter. My son definitely was a Master.

I could go on and on about the wonderful gifts given and received because of The Awakenings. Two of which happened not very long ago.

One occurred while I was attending an Intensive here in Colorado, given by Jim Solo, who is also a Master of Awakenings. I was on the table, and we were just getting into the Awakening when a voice spoke to me, coming from someplace other than the room we were in.

It said, "Child, how can I give unto you, if you are not willing to receive?" In my knowingness, I knew it was God speaking to me, and I also knew why. I have been one of so many who, during the course of my lifetime(s), especially this one, have been much more willing to give than to allow others to give to me. This usually comes from feeling non-deserving.

I then saw how really selfish this was of me—for I was denying others the pleasure of being able to give. I also was shown a picture of everyone wanting to give, but no one willing to receive—how frustrating that would be. Lesson given, lesson learned.

Another time, after receiving an Awakening from my dearest friend, Gary, a wondrous gift was given to me which I gratefully acknowledged. We were in the hot tub, just enjoying the beautiful night. The stars were out in all their glory, not a cloud in the sky.

Gary was sitting across from me in the tub and, like me, was gazing up at the sky. The next thing I knew, a silvery mist started forming itself into branches, and surrounded me, emerging from the trunk of a huge tree. The branches were so thick and heavy with silvery leaves that they were bending down all around me, and felt moist against my face.

There was so much energy within them that I knew that this was not a normal tree of the Earth, but something from a much higher level. Besides, there were no trees even close to the tub. Feeling a very high vibration of love, I remember saying over and over, "Thank you, thank you, thank you." I looked over to where Gary was and saw him drinking in that energy, using his hands to pull it into him.

Suddenly it started dissipating, but just before it disappeared, I received this message: *"This is the tree of life. Within it lies all understanding, all compassion, all knowledge, all forgiveness, all joy, all ecstasy and all love. Drink deeply of its nectar and the illusion will be no more."* Then all was gone, leaving me sitting across from Gary in the hot tub as a million and one stars twinkled high above.

Yes, the Awakenings are a wonderful way to raise awareness and vibration. However, each individual must find his/her own special path, using whatever calls to them—i.e., different strokes for different folks.

So I continue giving Awakenings and doing my energy work, releasing entities that have attached themselves to those who have lowered their vibration through drugs and negative thinking. Thus the person receives a much higher vibration and understanding, for they are no longer being controlled by those who should have gone on. It also releases the entity as well, so it can get on with its life.

Those old, unwanted, negative feelings of guilt, fears, self-doubts, self blame, judgments are also released and replaced with love and light. All of this can happen in one Awakening. However, it takes whatever it takes. It all has to do with how clear we already are, and how willing we are to face our judgments. And it is always within the guidance of the Awakenee's Whole Soul Self.

Once all of this "gunk" comes off, then the vibration of the person rises noticeably. They begin loving themselves without judgment, and everything around them. Life becomes more interesting, not so traumatic, and things start going right. They also find that others are responding to them in a more loving and supportive manner. Abandonment issues no longer exist.

Awakenings can be very subtle. However, they will continue reverberating throughout the individual's universe, as well as those within that reality, thus expanding the awareness long after the session is over. I have seen couples become more loving, families reunited. I have also seen couples split up—their vibration was no longer compatible, or perhaps it never was, at least for a long-term relationship.

However, when awareness is brought to a higher state, decisions can be made with more regard for all concerned. All of this will have a domino effect throughout the planet. Every time we take a step upward in our awareness, it also helps to raise awareness around us, thus setting in motion a wave of higher vibration.

As love and awareness comes in, one then becomes more of the Light, dissipating the darkness within. Thus the dramatizations of past judgments fade away, leaving you operating in present time. This is very important, for when one operates in the moment, then all of their attention units are focused upon what is happening in the present. Thus important decisions can be made quickly, with a clear mind and in the best interest of all.

It also aligns all of your bodies so that each one is vibrating in unison with the other and, of course, the higher the better. This will then create peace within, healing body, mind and spirit, and will also heal our beautiful Mother Earth, for we are Her children.

None of us are the same, for we are all uniquely different. Yet, on the other hand, we all are one in our search for that certain thing which will catapult us into the awareness of who we really are—into our Signature Vibration.

LOOK UPON EVERYTHING

THROUGH THE EYES OF LOVE

AND

BEHOLD LIFE'S
AWESOME BEAUTY

WENDING MY WAY TO PAONIA

Golden aspen leaves are dancing
Shimmering in the sun
A winding mountain trail calls follow me
Snow-capped mountains touch the sky
A little brook goes laughing by
Like them, I'm feeling wild, feeling free

For this is Colorado, Colorado you're my home
And here is where I want to be
As snow-capped mountains touch the sky
A Golden Eagle goes soaring by
Weaving its magic spell around me
Then with the Eagle, I soar free

It was September and fall was in the air. My roommate, with whom I shared a two-bedroom house in Santa Fe, was smoking pot, big time. Her energies were very unbalanced—literally driving me nuts.

I went out for breakfast, as usual, and received this message: "Pack your bag and leave the area." Since this seemed an exciting, as well as an excellent idea, I did just that. Throwing a few things in a bag, I put my Awakening table and some of my most powerful and favorite crystals in the trunk of Starfire, my trusty little Subaru, and hit the road.

I didn't have the slightest notion as to where this day would lead me. However, being one of those cock-eyed optimists who loves to do things on the spur of the moment, it didn't really matter. So, putting some distance between Santa Fe and myself, I arrived at the little town of Pagosa Springs, just on the border of Colorado and New Mexico.

After an early lunch, I proceeded up Wolf Creek Pass, which had been portrayed in a song and has always intrigued me. The words in the song didn't really describe the beauty that opened up before me.

I felt so wonderfully in "synch" with the surroundings of tall mountains, beautiful evergreens rising to the sky, sparkling streams tumbling down the mountainside. Peace and quiet was everywhere—filling my very soul with its wonderful healing energies.

Coming upon a little town nestled high in the mountains, surrounded by numerous lakes, I thought of staying there. Evidently that was not part of my itinerary, so I continued down a graveled road until reaching a main highway. A huge dam spread out in front of me with two signs. One sign pointed to Gunnison with the other toward Montrose.

Gunnison didn't feel right to me, so I opted to go in the direction of Montrose. However, that was not my point of destination either. Nearing the end of the dam, I noticed a small road circling around the end of it. It seemed to be calling me to follow, so I did.

There was a feeling of excitement, like a kid who had just discovered a new path through the forest. I was on a two-lane paved road, winding its way along the side of a canyon which got deeper and darker the farther I went.

The higher I went, the more spectacular the view. Finally, I just had to stop and get out of the confinement of my car. The scenery was breathtaking, and seeing it from the windows of my car was, to me, unthinkable.

Pulling over at the first opportunity, I got out and walked to the edge for a better look-see. The contrast of the brilliant blue sky with a few white fluffy clouds floating above me, and the deep canyon shadowed with dark green trees gave it the appearance of being almost black at the bottom.

To add to this magical scene, the Gunnison River was like a silvery thread of light plunging and twisting its way toward its own destination. I had discovered the Black Canyon of the Gunnison, which since has been made a National Monument.

Standing there, mesmerized, something told me to look up. There, slowly circling above me was a beautiful golden eagle adding even more magic to my already magical experience.

"Ah, Spirit, I do thank you for bringing me here," I whispered. I didn't know what lay ahead, but knew whatever it was would be perfect, for the golden eagle is always a good omen for me. It is the most powerful of my power animals, and has always been with me.

By now the sun was beginning to set and the dark canyon was becoming even darker. Not knowing where I was nor how far I would have to travel before reaching a town, I continued on my way. By now the top of the canyon had flattened out as small ranches came into view.

Finally, coming upon a small town with very few stores, I thought, "this might be a place for me to stay for the night." However, there was no room at the inn—in fact, there wasn't even an inn, it was that small. Upon asking, I was told that a larger town was only 11 miles on down the road.

By now it was getting dark, so on I sped. Sure enough, the next town was larger with motels and restaurant. So, I spent my first night in Hotchkiss. Its energy didn't really call to me, so early the next morning I found myself on the road again, heading for a town called Paonia.

I never saw the town, but passed a neat little motel with a rather large, impressive restaurant. The sign said "Redwood Arms Motel." It called to me, but ignoring the call, I decided to revisit Glenwood Springs. So, over McClure Pass I went, which was no smuck when it came to delivering beautiful, eye-popping scenery.

I pulled into Glenwood Springs, expecting to feel that high energy I had experienced some 30 years earlier, when I would go up to soak in its wonderful hot springs. However, either my or its energy had changed, drastically—probably both, for a lot of water had gone down the pike since that time.

It was overrun with people. The town, which at one time was charming and magical, was now, to me, just another town bursting at its seams with tourists. I felt that their energies were too varied and different to be compatible with mine. Disappointed, I wanted to leave, but wasn't certain where to go or what to do.

However, that was short-lived, for the memory of that little Redwood Arms Motel and the peace I felt around that area flashed across my mind. So, turning Starfire around, back I went.

Registering at the little motel, I unpacked, went to the restaurant and had a wonderful dinner. Everything seemed so right, the motel, the restaurant and the energies made me feel almost like I was home. I decided to make this my headquarters while exploring the mountains around me. Once again I was happy and thankful for having listened to my guides.

Early the next morning, I ate breakfast at the breakfast shop next door. The owner and those eating there were very friendly and helpful, giving me information regarding some of the most scenic areas to explore. I decided to explore Kebler Pass.

Retracing the route I had taken the day before to go to Glenwood Springs, I turned off onto a graveled road as directed.

The trip up the Black Canyon had been awesome. However, this time I was in for a special treat. Instead of dark and shadowy, the mountains seemed to be ablaze with color. Colorado had exchanged her green wardrobe for her most radiant fall attire, and the high mountain pass was the perfect place to get a panoramic view.

The deep green of the spruce enhanced the brilliant reds of the underbrush while golden aspen leaves shimmered and danced in the brilliant sun.

A few deer crossed my path, as well as chipmunks. Rounding a curve, there on a rock, sunning themselves, were two beautiful marmots. Everything seemed so magical. It was as though I had stepped into another world—a world more compatible to my own vibration.

I spent the entire day driving, getting out often to snap pictures and drink in the beauty. Finally, I arrived at what appeared to be the top of the pass, where a very old graveyard silently called to me.

It belonged to a town that had evidently been abandoned, and had been reclaimed by Mother Earth—at least I never found it. However, since I love exploring old graveyards and reading the inscriptions on the tombstones, I did just that.

Sometimes, while doing this, I will feel the energy of a spirit that has not gone on, but has become earth-bound. When I do, I immediately work with the energy to release it to the Light—if it wishes to go. However, I didn't feel anything but peace and quietness. So it was apparent that was not the reason I was there.

I walked around, reading the inscriptions—some dating back into the 1800s. All were very interesting. It gave me a sort of connection and I found myself wondering what their lives had been like back then.

One little grave was of a very young child. What grief and heartache that must have caused its parents. But life in its many forms goes on, unfolding and evolving on its path to the Light.

By now it was getting late, so I turned Starfire around and headed back to my room. Showering the day's energies off, I put on fresh clothes and decided to find that little town they called Paonia.

I didn't have long to travel—about a quarter of a mile—and there was the sign, which I had missed before. Turning off on the side road, which was dotted with houses, I came to a stop sign. I was in the middle of Paonia.

On the right side was a restaurant named The Cave. I was going to turn and go in. However, the message was very clear for me to turn left. Upon doing so, I noticed another restaurant. So, parking, I went inside.

Walking through the door, I saw that there was a bar with some booths further back. There was quite a lot of talking going on, and I wasn't certain whether to go in there or into the quiet little dining area just to my right. I thought that I would prefer its peace and quiet to the noisier one. However, the message was very clear and precise—GO WHERE THE ACTION Is! So I did.

Seating myself in the booth directly in front of the three, a man and two women, who were talking up a storm, I pretended not to be listening to their conversation. However, when I heard them discussing the possibility of starting a Healing Light Center, I dropped all pretenses and started talking to them. I told them I was from Santa Fe and had been guided to come to Paonia.

They were highly interested in hearing about the Awakenings, and asked me to join them. This I did, for I was as eager to connect with them as they were with me.

Before leaving, I had gotten their names and phone numbers. Soupy, the man, had made arrangements to come to my motel room the next morning to experience an Awakening. To say the least, I was thrilled and thanked Spirit profusely for guiding me to where they were.

Soupy arrived on schedule the next day. I had set up my table with crystals and candles, and was ready when he arrived. It turned out to be a magical Awakening. He gifted me more than I usually get and was on his way back home. The others came to me later for an Awakening, after I had moved to Paonia.

This cinched it for me. I didn't know how I was going to move to this place, but I was never more certain in my life that this was to be my next home.

I stayed on a couple of more days and met up with Ann, who published The Star Beacon, and had the kind of vibration I was searching for when I left Santa Fe. She and her soul mate, Ethan, were and still are wonderful friends.

However, it was time for me to return to Santa Fe, so back I went. I spent the rest of the winter in New Mexico, doing Awakenings, traveling around the area and staying wherever I could. My roommate and I had parted company, so wherever I hung my hat was home during those months.

Spring was turning into summer and once again I felt the pull to revisit Paonia and check it out one more time before moving. Besides, I didn't know if there would be a place available that I could afford.

Driving into the area, once again I felt that wonderful "I am home" feeling. So I checked into the little motel, and decided to find a place to live. There was no doubt in my mind that the right one would appear. However, upon talking to a real estate man who just happened to be having breakfast the same time I was, left me wondering if I wasn't completely "off my rocker."

He said that there just weren't any available rentals in my price range. Then, suddenly, he reversed his statement and said, "Oh, by the way, a friend of mine just bought a little duplex across from the Town Park. Would you be interested in seeing it?"

Would I? I wanted to go right then and meet the owner. He said he would have to set up an appointment, which he did, and I connected with the owner, Steve, that afternoon.

The little duplex was old but nice. It was a one-bedroom with a bath, kitchen and good-sized living room—plenty large enough to hold my few belongings, for I had lightened the load considerably before moving to Santa Fe.

Paying the month's rent and security deposit, off I went to get my son, Jimmy, who was once again residing in Taos in his large converted school bus. Together, with help from friends, we loaded my things into the bus and, with Starfire leading the way, caravaned back to Paonia, taking the less mountainous route.

When I had talked to my new landlord earlier, he told me that I could have the dresser and large mirror to use that was in the other side of the duplex. There was also a kitchen table with two chairs, and one rather comfortable living room chair.

Setting up my Awakening table in the bedroom, I decided to sleep on it until a more suitable daybed for the living room could be found. When I realized that there was no bed for me to sleep on, I remembered a very funny incident, which made me laugh. "What's so funny, Mom?" Jimmy asked.

"I was thinking of the time I was getting rid of most of my furniture in Glendale, remember?"

"Yeah, you sure didn't want to give up that big bed, did you?" he replied, laughing. It had happened when I was getting ready to leave that area. Bashar had told us to start "lightening the load." So before leaving Glendale, I did just that.

Jimmy was helping me with selling most of the furniture, which I had dragged from my Phoenix home to my Burbank, California home, and then, after selling both of them, crammed everything into my apartment in Glendale, another suburb of Los Angeles.

The only thing I really didn't want to sell was my queen-sized bed with its wonderful mattress. I had run an ad, and was selling practically all of my furniture. When it came time for my bed to go, I burst into tears.

Jimmy, puzzled at this outburst, asked, "Well, do you want to sell it or not?" He was just ready to close the deal.

I looked at my bed and then my guides took over—they can be so wonderful in decision making. "I don't know," I blubbered, tears streaming down my cheeks.

Just then, I got this ridiculous picture of me going down the highway in my little Renault—and I do mean little—the big box springs and the mattress precariously perched on top. You could hardly see the little car for the oversized bed. The picture was so comical that I started to laugh. Jimmy looked at me in surprise—he probably thought I had finally lost all of my marbles. I said, "Sell it."

Later I told him what I had been shown, and we both had a good chuckle over the incident. My guides never cease to amaze me. I never know to what length they will go to get me out of a situation I no longer need to be in.

So once again we had a good laugh as Jimmy and I finished unpacking my things. The couple who had rented the other side also helped us. We hung pictures and made the little place more livable.

Then came the Fourth of July. I was getting ready to do an Awakening on Jimmy when, all of a sudden, the whole area started filling up with people. A big parade was about to begin—drums, marching band, horses, old cars and all—and it was coming right down the street, passing by the duplex where I lived. The park was its destination.

Knowing that an Awakening would be impossible with all that noise and assorted energies, I canceled the Awakening and fixed breakfast. Jimmy and I ate while we watched from our kitchen window as the parade went marching by. The view couldn't have been more perfect.

"Just look at all those beautiful horses," I told Jimmy.

"What horses? I'm looking at the beautiful girls," he replied. Oh well, to each his own.

That night we watched a wonderful display of fireworks as we sat on the deck attached to my duplex. We both joked about how wonderful it was to receive such a welcome from the little town—just like we were celebrities or someone of great importance.

It was time for Jimmy to return to Taos, so the next morning he left in his bus and I followed him on the excuse that I wanted to make certain he made it back without any bus breakdowns. The truth of the matter was, I just wanted to spend as much time as possible with my son and my dog, Thor, who was traveling with Jimmy at that time.

Upon returning to my new little home, I busied myself doing Awakenings and getting acquainted. Ann and I started a Sunday brunch meeting, where a group of like-minded people would meet and talk about extra-terrestrial happenings and sightings of UFOs. I traveled back and forth from Paonia to Crestone, Colorado, doing my work. Jimmy was now living in Crestone, having moved from Taos shortly after I moved to Paonia.

Crestone is also very beautiful and mystical, but for some reason it never called to me to settle there like Paonia did. Evidently I was to be in Paonia for a reason. I felt so nurtured, so at home there.

Little did I know that I was being prepared and strengthened for an ordeal, which I soon was going to be forced to face.

take the judgment off and look upon
everything as being perfect in
every moment just the way it is

for judgment creates karma if there is no
judgment there will be no Karma

WE NEVER SAID GOODBYE

How can the pieces all come together
After they've fallen apart
Blown by life's winds and scattered
Each taking a piece of my heart

Beautiful, painful memories
Returning again to haunt me
What are they trying to tell me
What am I really to see

Somewhere there must be a lesson
For me to find—understand
When will the loneliness vanish
And the picture made whole in my hand

But how can it all come together
I don't even know where to start
Then my answer became so very clear
The journey begins in your heart

It seems as though there is no permanency in anything. You touch someone's life or they yours, and when you look around they no longer are there. Only the bittersweet memory remains.

In one sense this is true, for we are always changing form. However, the essence of who we truly are remains the same. We may have lost a mate, a child, a friend, parents, a loved one through their transformation, but as time goes on, we do meet up with them again and sometimes in the most unusual and unexpected ways.

Have you ever met someone for the first time, and there is something so familiar about them that you would swear you know them, but can't quite nail it down? There is an old song that ends with this haunting question, "But who knows where or when?"

This has happened to me many times this lifetime. It wasn't until I started to wake up to the truth of life that I became aware that some of these people, who are touching my life here and now, are the same ones who have shared a lifetime or lifetimes with me before this one.

Some of those lifetimes may or may not have had a fairy tale existence. I have discovered that if I get a feeling of instant dislike or uneasiness regarding a person when we first meet, then I'll lay you odds that there has been some dastardly deeds done, probably on both sides.

It never is one-sided, even if we like to pretend that it is. Some call it karma, but all we really have to know is that the judgment we place upon a situation is what creates our karma. Remove the judgment and you'll remove the karma. Yes, it can be that simple, unless we choose to hang onto and dramatize the illusion, but why keep dredging up the past, unless you love being miserable? Once the judgment has been removed, the past can have no claim on you.

Then there is the other side of the coin, meeting someone and, wham bam, you're thrown for a loop. Feelings run high, passions soar and almost irresistible urges rise within you to be with this person, no matter the cost.

This can lead to a very interesting relationship. It usually stems from sharing a lifetime, which was never quite finished. The curtain went down before the final scene was allowed to play out.

And so the game goes on until we finally wake up and discover that we have been trying to relive a past life instead of creating one in the now.

Once we see beyond the illusion of these emotions, we can then start creating our relationships in the present. There are, however, some long-standing relationships that may be a forever commitment, such as soul mates or twin flames.

I am sure we have all had this kind of a connection—a feeling so deep, so powerful that you feel that it has always been and always will be. That no matter what happens, you must stand by, protecting and assisting—to be with this person at all cost.

You may not like what is happening and you may even swear that "this is the last time," but deep down you know you are only kidding yourself. There really is no other choice. The commitment was made, and until that commitment is finalized there is no other way to go.

You can, through agreement, walk away, but there still is a feeling of unfinished business. You then will eventually find yourself coming back, checking in to make certain all is well. It may be the same or another lifetime. Of course, this is also true of the other one—you check in with them and vice versa.

This was the case with the one whom I call Jimmy. This lifetime he was my son, but there were many other lifetimes we were together. It never is one-sided, where one does all the giving, and the other the receiving. The scales may tip one way or the other each lifetime, but who keeps score? What really counts in the final analysis is the love we have shared and the lessons learned.

With the sound of a gunshot exploding in my ears, I awoke from a dream that had turned into a horrible nightmare. Only it wasn't a dream, it was real, it had happened. This was the fifth night that as soon as I closed my eyes, I would begin reliving every heart-rendering, terrifying moment, almost to the last detail, which always ended with the explosion of the gun.

First I would see the converted bus that he had driven to the border of California and Mexico. Police surrounding the bus, trying to talk him out of killing himself, thus making the situation worse. I could feel his pain, his anger, his confusion, and his fear. The final feelings that I would feel were a sort of desperation and resignation to the fact that it was time to end it all. Then, with the sound of the gun being fired, all feelings, emotions, et cetera, would end and I would be left, wide awake, shaking with the painful knowingness that this wasn't a dream.

Lying there, wide-awake, I started recalling the day it happened, and the call from the sheriff the next day. I remembered how, on that fateful Sunday, I had felt so upset, knowing that something was wrong.

I always knew when Jimmy was in trouble. He was so much a part of me that I could feel his feelings, his thoughts. This day was no different. I wanted to go to him, find him, but he had distanced himself so that this time there was to be no interference with his destiny.

So I paced the floor in my little apartment, trying to figure out how I could find him. I felt desperate, scattered, unable to think. Wanting to run to him, but wasn't certain where he was.

I knew he was on his way to his land in the Baja Peninsula in Mexico and that he was somewhere near the border in California.

Calling my brother in San Diego, I told him of my concern. He said that he and his wife, Kathy, would drive up to where I thought Jimmy was on Tuesday, and see if they could find him and give him some moral support.

All day Sunday I waited by the phone, nervously pacing the floor, knowing that something was terribly wrong. Later Sunday night a very peaceful feeling came over me, and I went to bed, sleeping soundly.

The next morning there was no anxiety, just a calm, peaceful feeling which lasted all day until around 4 p.m., when I received the call. It was the sheriff telling me as gently as possible that my son had shot himself the day before.

I remembered screaming, "No! No! Please, I don't want to hear it. Are you sure? It can't be him."

"Is Jim Prescott your son?" he asked.

When I answered yes, he verified that it was true. My son was dead. Later I recalled how upset I had been all day Sunday, and the peaceful feeling I felt later that night—about the time he shot himself. I now know that I was with him right to the end.

So here I was, wide awake again. Enough is enough, I muttered to myself as I got up, went to my little kitchen table where I had set up an altar with candles, crystals, and a picture of Lord Jesus. I had created this when I received word that Jimmy's ashes would be arriving.

Once again I lit the candles, picked up the box that contained his ashes. Holding it close to my heart, I rocked back and forth. It seemed almost as if I, once again, was holding that tiny baby who I so often had held and rocked to sleep.

"Dear God, is this all that is left of my son, just a box of ashes?" I sobbed. As the sobbing subsided, I started remembering the day he left. He was so happy, so full of expectation.

I had accompanied him in my car to Grand Junction, where he stopped to fill up with gas. He hugged me but never said goodbye. "See you in the spring, Mom," he called over his shoulder as he climbed into his bus.

"I can hardly wait," I called back, waving to him as he drove out of sight. I did some shopping, then went back to Paonia and Thor, my beautiful Rottweiler-Doberman that Jimmy had brought back to be with me. Thor was my dog, but he also was Jimmy's. He was a part of our connection, like a link of the chain of love that held us together.

I remember Jimmy saying, "Mom, you had better keep Thor this time. He's getting too old to go on such long trips." I now know that he knew, on some level, what was going to happen. That I would need Thor, who was and still is a guide, a teacher and a wonderful companion.

How many times has this happened, I wondered, when we never had the chance to say goodbye? I remembered a past life that I had been shown several years earlier while sitting in my apartment in Glendale, Calif. I was looking out of my large window at a brilliant blue sky when suddenly a scene started unfolding.

I seemed to be on a different planet than Earth. Spirit later told me that at the time of that scenario, I was on Orion. It seemed very barren, sandy. I was alone, watching and waiting for something or someone. It was quite breezy and I could see my dress or tunic swirling around my legs.

Suddenly a small spacecraft appeared, landing a short distance from me. I ran toward it as a tall, handsome man climbed down, and held out his arms to me. We embraced, but seemed to be rather fearful and apprehensive.

I handed him some sort of a packet, which he slipped inside his uniform. We quickly embraced and he climbed back into his craft. I saw myself standing there, waving and watching as it rose into the sky.

He had gone only a short distance when the craft exploded. I watched, horrified, as burning pieces fell to the ground.

Much later I was given the information that we both were in the service for the underground, fighting the tyranny of the dark rulers, and that I had given him important secret documents.

I was a spy working inside the ruling government in order to further the underground's fight for freedom. Later I was caught and put to death. So that was the first time that I ever remembered being with this one whom I knew this lifetime as my son, Jimmy. And that time, like this, we never said goodbye.

We have spent many lifetimes together here on planet Earth, but knowing this still didn't take away the pain of losing him this time.

Exhausted from so much emotional turmoil, I blew out the candles and went to bed. Dropping off to sleep almost immediately, I slept peacefully through what was left of the night.

The nightmare never returned, but Jimmy did, many times, to assist me through that difficult period of his transition. He was, for me, a teacher, as I was for him. He taught me many things, both before and after he left the planet.

Shortly after this happened, I received the money order back that I had sent after we had talked on the phone.

He was a wonderful silversmith, but his jewelry wasn't selling and he was getting pretty broke. So he gave me the name of the town that he would soon be in and I sent the money, general delivery, in care of that post office.

I found myself shaking as I opened up the envelope, for I already knew what it contained. My judgment was coming up, big time. I started sobbing. "Damn it all, Jimmy," I sobbed. "I couldn't even do that much for you."

Suddenly his voice came in, just as clear as though he were standing there in person talking to me, and I heard him say, *It's no biggy, little Mommy. Take the judgment off, it's perfect just the way it is.*

My sobs turned to laughter as I recognized the truth of what he was saying. My judgment of not helping him lifted and I felt a wonderful, warm, loving energy surrounding me. There was no doubt that the voice I heard was his. He was still teaching me, for that was one of his favorite sayings—take the judgment off, it's perfect, just the way it is. Of course, this is always true when we start looking upon everything as a learning experience.

I, of course, continued releasing and letting go of my grief, my self-judgment and anger. I recall one evening while sitting in a restaurant in the little town of Paonia, where I resided. It was almost dark and I was feeling the emotions of anger, sadness, grief and loneliness rising up in me. I received some kind of a message to go for a drive—to leave the restaurant. So, paying for my coffee, I got into my car and started up Stevens Gulch.

I hadn't driven very far when my anger came up. I really cut loose, cussing Jimmy, God, the situation, myself, and everything else I could think of. It was "Katie bar the door." I remember shouting at the top of my lungs words that would make a sea pirate blush. Then, when the anger subsided, I started sobbing.

By this time I had parked the car, knowing that I would be unable to drive with all those emotions coming up.

Suddenly the illusion gave way and I saw death for what it was—a transformation, an evolvement of life into another expression of itself. I started laughing. Once again I felt that beautiful peace come over me. Tears and laughter do work wonders in assisting one in releasing their pain. I started the car, turned it around, still laughing.

Once again I heard Jimmy's voice, asking, "Feeling better, little Mommy?" This made me laugh even harder, for I knew, beyond a shadow of a doubt, that he was with me and would remain until I had worked through this traumatic and painful time. There was also the knowingness that we never would have to say goodbye. That there really was no separation—never had been, for that is only a part of the illusion. Love is the glue that holds us together, not for one lifetime, but forever.

Another time that I remembered so vividly was when I had taken Thor for a walk in the mountains. I was into my stuff, and Thor was not being too cooperative in minding me. In fact, he was being a butt-head.

I had turned him loose and he decided to take off up the mountain, leaving me behind. I went into fear of "what if something happens to him; what if he gets hurt or disappears, and I don't know how to find him to help him?" Almost the same exact thoughts and fears I had that Sunday when Jimmy left the planet. I was practically in tears.

"Damn it, Jimmy," I said. "Why did you have to leave him with me, anyway?"

I heard Jimmy's voice laughingly answer, Someone had to be here to bring up your stuff, since I wasn't going to be with you anymore.

I started laughing, Thor appeared, almost instantly, and we continued our walk. Jimmy and Thor have always been very adept at teaching me Unconditional Love with no judgment, no matter what the situation.

Believe me, when we come to the complete understanding that death is only a transformation and that there really is no separation, it is a wonderful realization. This, in turn, breaks through the illusion that we cannot see or be in touch with our loved ones who have gone on. So rise above the illusion of death and allow yourself to see the truth. See with your heart, not with your mind, and the truth will set you free.

I'm not saying that losing someone through the experience of death is not traumatic. Allow yourself with love to experience the emotional feelings of loss, grief and anger.

Then, when it is time, you will come to know the peace, the joy and will see past the illusion, the dramatization that we have so solidly bought into. This was one of Lord Jesus' many teachings, *Death is an illusion. Life is everlasting.*

There are many stories I could tell you about Jimmy's returning to assist me, keeping in touch. Some may appear from time to time within this book.

However, the bottom line is that this is not just about me, for I am only one of the characters in this big play we call life. The ones that we lose through their transformation will, if allowed, return to assist us through our grief, anger and judgment, as will our angels and guides.

All we have to do is to see with our hearts and believe, for believing is seeing. When you feel you have to see in order to believe, you are in your head. When you believe with your heart, that is when you will truly see. Then the universe will open its doors unto you, and all will be revealed. This is the promise and God does not lie.

*whenever you find you are judging a
scenario of the past ask yourself
"if given the chance would I do it
differently so as to change the outcome"
If your answer is "I most certainly would
change the outcome" then thank yourself
for the lesson learned and move on
Otherwise you may find yourself
recreating that scenario all over again.*

HAUNTING MEMORIES

Shadowy figures laughing at me, playing with my insanity

Many voices speak to us from out of the past. This is because they have been encased in a cocoon of guilt and self-judgment, hidden from our consciousness. So they keep knocking at our door, bringing up our fears and judgments.

At first, I was not even aware of why they were there, or what they were trying to show me. I felt life would be so much simpler if they would just go away. However, no matter how hard I tried to push them back down, they were persistent; seemingly out of nowhere they would appear to haunt me again.

I didn't want to look at them, let alone own up to the fact that I would ever be a part of, nor have anything to do with such "dastardly deeds." However, the more I tried to shut them out, the more persistent they became and the more I judged them.

What you resist will persist is so true. Thus I kept on creating more of the kind of scenarios that would cause more guilt and self-blame.

This would blow everything out of proportion—like building mountains out of molehills. Then up would come my old stubborn "I have to be right, no matter what" syndrome, and off I'd go again, creating other scenarios of like substance in order to prove that I was right. Of course, I always failed—there is no wrong or right when judgment is removed. Judgment always sends one further out of their true balance of love and harmony. And so the merry-go-round ride continued, as around and around I'd go, locked into my own habitual-ritual scenarios.

Of course, like many, I tried to excuse my actions by blaming others for causing it to happen. This seldom, if ever, works. "They co-created the scenario, so it's their fault, thus I was the victim," I tried telling myself, and that old excuse "the devil made me do it" didn't work either, at least not for me.

I now have come to realize that it isn't what others do to us, but rather what we do to others that sets up our judgments. The bottom line is always what we have done either to others or ourselves. When we look at the bigger picture, it always boils down to this equation: "What we do to others, or allow others to do to us, we also do to ourselves"—*the Law of ONE.*

The responsibility always lies within each of us—what we choose to create for our lessons. Thus we are fragmented, until we get the reason why we allowed ourselves to experience it in the first place. When we do, we then take a step upward in our awareness. Each step takes us closer to becoming whole as we reunite with the many fragmented parts of ourselves. Reliving the past has been a very painful time for me. Facing what I have done to others, and also to myself, was hard to come to grips with. I have now come to realize that with this pain also came the knowledge and understanding necessary to open up

No longer will I commit to creating or co-creating something I feel is not for my own or others' highest good. Once realizing that it was a co-creation for all who participated in order to experience and evolve has made it more palatable and easier to confront.

Many are the times that I have wished that I could go back and undo the pain and unhappiness I co-created with others. However, I know that is impossible, and so I accept that fact. Yet deep within me lies the feeling of wishing to create that scenario in a more loving and meaningful way.

"Backward oh backward, oh time in your flight;" if only I had the power to return to those days of yore, things would be much different. Of course, I would want to do this only if I could use the knowledge gleaned from what I have experienced. Otherwise it would be the same thing all over again.

For starters, I would choose a mate of a higher vibration, more compatible with my own. My children would be raised in a home of love, compassion and understanding instead of utter chaos and confusion. They would be taught to love themselves, unconditionally, in order to make the right choices for their highest evolvement, and a smoother path.

Mother would have lived her last days in a loving and nurturing atmosphere instead of spending them in grief and heartache. And I would also have had a more enjoyable life. However, everything was perfect for each of us in that particular time, when not looked at through the eyes of judgment.

Now I am not saying that all of those different scenarios, which I, and the others, co-created were not for our highest good. (As you probably have noticed, I always say I first, which is not proper grammar. However, it does point out that I, in my reality, was always in the driver's seat for my own part of co-creating any and all scenarios. Thus showing that I take full responsibility for my creations.)

Each of us did put ourselves in direct contact with the other in order to experience what we, from the viewpoint of our Higher Guidance, felt we needed for growth and evolvement. Yet, no matter how I try, I still can't imagine an angel like my mother having to experience her last days in such a way as she did.

However, that which I would now create, was not a part of our paths at that time. So no longer will I allow myself to dwell on what might have been. The reality is that it happened within the Illusion's game on Planet Earth, and I refuse to return to that low vibration ever again.

Having been there, done that, I now have risen to the awareness that I no longer need those experiences for my evolvement. In realizing this, I have let it all go with a thankful heart for all of the experiences, and also for those who assisted me on this rocky path I chose to walk.

I, and I along, put myself in those scenarios of creating and co-creating. It was my choice and no one else's. Realizing that it was all in the game of experiencing and learning has freed me from my judgment, thus making it a lot easier for me to face me.

Since releasing my guilt and blame, I have taken full responsibility, owning my own part in whatever scenario my judgments had stuck me. It matters not a whit to me who did what to whom. I know that I was supposed to be a part of that scenario, or I wouldn't have been there. And now, knowing that all experiences are for our evolvement, I thank any and all for whatever part they played.

My Mother of this lifetime was a beautiful, giving person. She never complained, taking Dad's raving tantrums without letting on how much it hurt—at least not to us kids. She always saw everyone through the eyes of love, and, as far as I know, never said a bad thing about anyone.

Papa, as we called him, was not a mean person. Now upon looking back, I know that he was confused, frightened and sometimes felt overwhelmed with trying to eke out a living for the family. Mother seemed to understand this, and thus supported him in all ways.

He would, when stressed, blow up, loudly blaming her for spending too much money on food, even though she stretched every penny to the limit in order to feed and clothe her family.

He also was extremely jealous, which tells me that he was also very insecure within himself. Now I have compassion and understanding, where I used to have confusion and anger regarding him. I'm certain that neither one's life was a bed of roses, but is anyone's?

I know that it hasn't been for any of my family. My two brothers and older sister and I all grew up rather lopsided. I was the youngest of the lot. My two brothers were quite successful at making a far better-than-average living. They each had a more or less inflated ego.

My sister and I were just the opposite, very insecure with deflated ones. The two boys seemed to be the apple of both Mother's and Dad's eyes, while we girls were just girls, or so it seemed to me.

My sister died at a relatively early age from misusing instead of loving her body. Cigarettes, booze and loneliness were the main culprits. However, the doctor said it was emphysema, which brought on a heart attack. I know it was her own sort of suicide—all death is.

Were I to do it, I would choose a less painful exit, but to each her/his own. I trust her next journey on Planet Earth will be less traumatic.

My two brothers are nearing the end of their roller-coaster ride. Having experienced, I trust, that they have also learned much.

My older brother became a general contractor, and my younger one became a senior airline pilot. They both were quite successful in their chosen fields as far as money and prestige was concerned.

However, they each experienced what an unbalanced ego can create. The younger one became addicted to alcohol after retiring as a senior captain from the airlines—his poor ego just couldn't handle not being the top banana anymore. He was a baritone, and his glorious voice was lost in all that alcohol. He had so much going for him but, as they say, "that's life."

My older brother was a reflection of our father and treated his wife accordingly. He had a lot of deep anger, but never bothered to explore the whys or wherefores of it. He rode the waves of success and then lost most of his money in a bad business venture.

His wife died of cancer. He literally has been brought to his knees and has become very much involved with his church. He has since remarried, but is still the same—deeply disturbed, unhappy, controlling.

As for myself, well I, for some wonderful reason, took another path all together and am very happy that I found it. However, it hasn't been a bed of roses for me either.

My emotional body was very shut down when my sister died, so I didn't feel much loss. She had been taking care of Mother ever since Dad passed over, so now it was my turn.

I went back to Denver, and brought Mother back to Phoenix to live with me. Had I known then what was to transpire between the two of us, I would have made other arrangements, but that was not to be.

Mother did, what was for me at that time, the unforgivable thing—she got old. I sold the beautiful townhouse we had bought and dragged her off to California. She went along like a lamb to the slaughter. Never once complaining, just accepting.

At that time my communication and my compassion were so shut down that I never even bothered to talk it over with her or consider her feelings. With the help of my younger brother, we found a small house in the seedy part of Burbank.

I had asked him to do some research, which he and his alcoholic girl friend did. They must have really been boozed to the hilt. It was next to a freeway. The whole neighborhood left a lot to be desired. Of course, I didn't take responsibility either by checking out the neighborhood—another lesson of what happens when one does not take responsibility for one's self.

I sold our beautiful, quiet Phoenix home and took up residence in Burbank, spending most of my time elsewhere while Mother got older and more feeble. I had hired a woman to feed and look after her. However, I can't remember a time I even tried to carry on a conversation with her. What a lonely life that must have been for her.

Finally, it became apparent that she would have to go into a nursing home. So, again with the help of my brother, we chose one that now I wouldn't put my worst enemy into, let alone my beautiful mother.

We also had her beloved poodle put to sleep. Mother must have known what was about to happen, for she tried to let Flurry out of the car, telling her to run away. That's probably what she wanted to do, but couldn't.

My brother's now estranged wife came to see Mother, and was shocked at where we had put her. She tried to tell me how horrible it was. Even the owners asked me why Mother cried a lot. I was so tuned out, I didn't pay any attention to any of them.

Finally, Mother grew very weak. She had developed terrible bedsores. Our doctor put her in the hospital and she just faded away. She was buried beside Papa in Denver.

I never grieved. I was only relieved that she had at last left her bed of misery. I was still in Scientology at that time. It wasn't until I turned my back on them and was going to Bashar that I began to have some remorse regarding my treatment of Mother. Evidently the door to my emotional body was opening, slightly.

The voices were becoming insistent. What had I done? Why did I treat Mother that way? She had never been anything but a wonderful, caring Mother. I began remembering my visits to her in that awful home, and how guilty I would feel about her being there. When this would come up, I would immediately shut it off, and get away from that place as quickly as possible, leaving her behind in her misery and heartache.

However, the memories kept returning until the horror of what I had done to her were almost unbearable. No matter what I did, I couldn't escape those memories.

"I can't go on like this." I wanted to cry, but couldn't. I wanted to scream out, "Please forgive me," but she was no longer around to hear. I had only the judgments and the guilt of what I had done to comfort me, which were getting more and more out of control, spinning me into self-loathing.

Finally, in desperation, I packed a few things and left my Glendale apartment. I had sold our home after dumping Mother in that god-awful place.

Heading for the mountains, I knew that I was being guided by something or someone, and that I would somehow find a way to release this terrible guilt, self-loathing and anger. I was a volcano ready to explode.

I had learned rage therapy from Medicine Man Hawk, and knew that was what I was about to experience. And I was to "go it alone," or so I thought.

Rage therapy is done by taking an object, such as a pillow or some other object, and either beating on it or beating it against something else. This will allow the anger and self-judgments to rise up in the form of crying, cursing, or whatever. It does work wonders, and will release a lot of pent-up emotion, if one is willing to go that far.

I was more than willing to do anything to release the pain of my self-condemnation and guilt—but what was I to use?

I had parked the car on the side of a rather deserted road in the mountains, and had walked back into the forest where no one was even remotely close.

"Now, what's next?" I asked myself, for there was nothing around to assist me within eyesight. I thought of finding a branch or limb of a tree, but couldn't see any around.

Suddenly, a red-tailed hawk appeared directly in front of me. He'd fly just a little ways, then land. I felt the urge to follow him. He never seemed to go very far. It was as though he were guiding me, but to where or what, I wasn't certain.

I quickened my pace, not really knowing why, but felt he held the answer. He flew into a tree and seemed to be waiting for me.

Upon arriving to where he was, I looked down and there upon the ground was a rather large tree limb next to a big boulder. I knew I had been guided to the tools needed to perform the necessary and much-needed rage therapy.

Picking up the limb, I started pounding it against the rock. My self-loathing and anger were exploding. Every time I hit the rock, more would rise and release. The dam was breaking, as was the tree limb. It was almost in shreds.

Feeling tired and weak, I made my way down a short distance to another rock, which was next to a tree with low-hanging branches. I sat down, sobbing uncontrollably for a long time. Finally, a feeling of peace began replacing the anger and guilt.

I then had the feeling that I wasn't alone. Looking up at the tree branch just above me, I saw not one, but two beautiful red-tailed hawks. They seemed to be just sitting there, watching over me. I knew that they were my "animal guides."

Thanking them for their wonderful support as they flew away, I walked back to my car and returned home. The anger and most of the self-loathing was gone. However, time after time I would still get flashbacks of Mother, sobbing her heart out, alone in that horrible place.

Finally, I asked for help in releasing those memories. That was when I received this valuable lesson: I was asked, *"If you had the chance to relive that scenario with your Mother again, would you do it the same way?"*

"Of course not," I replied. "I wouldn't even think of doing such a thing."

"Then you have learned through this experience. Thank all who co-created this scenario with you, and remove the judgment."

This I did and felt that my Mother was smiling instead of crying. What a wonderful feeling—yes, I said feeling, for I was really starting to feel. My emotional body was opening up.

I could have learned a lot from my Mother and did, but was not aware of it until she was gone. However, I did learn, and now I know that our earthly encounters are sometimes of a higher nature than we can understand at the time. I know that she touched my life in a very special and loving way. I also have come to realize that she assisted me in co-creating that traumatic scenario, in order to bring me to the realization that my emotional body was really shut down. Thus began its healing.

Now, when I get into judgment, I let it go. That is what we should always do, for *Judgment Creates Karma*. If we don't have judgment, then there is no karma. We then are always in the now of each beautiful moment.

My Mother was the epitome of Unconditional Love. Thank you, dear one, for being my mother and reflecting to me your Unconditional Love. I thank Papa, too, for his part in the scenario of reflecting to me my other side—the anger, fear, and judgment—which I never explored until much later in my life.

I now see that the polarities reflected to me by both of them were a necessary part of my path. Thus I was drawn into that family unit, for we all choose those who will be of the greatest assistance for our earthly lessons. I needed both reflections for my evolvement and growth. Otherwise I may have never begun the journey of finding me, gathering my many fragmented parts along the way.

The Child Of Tears

While in my late teen-age years, I kept getting vivid pictures of a young child crying. I somehow felt connected to her, but didn't know why.

Who was she? Why was she so sad? She somehow gave me the feeling of being lost, abandoned. I could see her sitting by a window, alone and lonely, as if waiting for someone to come and comfort her.

She appeared quite often, and I would ponder over why I was seeing this child. This usually happened when I was feeling sad and lonely. I then would touch in on that vibration.

"Why am I seeing this?" I kept asking myself. Was she somehow trying to communicate to me, and for what reason? Then the picture would disappear. I would forget all about her, until the next time when she would flash through my mind.

It never seemed weird or anything. It did, however, leave me with an aching, lonely feeling, reflecting to me what I needed to explore, but chose to ignore.

These were some of the times that I would party, seek out companionship—anything to block out those feelings. This, of course, didn't work. It never does.

The pictures of the lost little girl finally dimmed, and then eventually disappeared altogether. However, I still had that lost feeling within.

It wasn't until I became aware of who that little child really was— not someone on the outside, lost within the dark, murky Illusion. She was the child within me, crying out for love and recognition.

This, of course, was my emotional body, which I had shut down, ignoring what I didn't want to face or recognize. However, when all of those haunting memories of this and other lifetimes started knocking at my door, I no longer could ignore them—they became very insistent.

There was no strong family unit within me for the child within— my emotional body—to share love with. The God/Goddess within (male/female) were completely ignoring each other and the child, each walled off from the other and myself, not able to share—to be a part of a loving family unit. Thus there was no real love for myself at that time

Of course, none of this was within my reality then. Yes, I really was fragmented, as are most people here on Planet Earth, all operating at a very low level of the totality of who they are.

My own two children were a perfect reflection of what was going on within me. However, back then, I was too blind to see.

When the child within is happily living within the confines of the heart by the side of our loving inner God/Goddess, then the feeling of peace and joy will vibrate within that person. This is when the imbalance within will leave, and in its place will come balance along with unconditional love and peace. It will then be reflected on the outside in like manner.

115

"A house divided against itself cannot stand" is true for each person. The separation within is reflected outside of oneself, thus we are seeing so many family units being split apart by this phenomenon.

When a person is completely within his/her own balance, i.e., God/Goddess/Child working as one unit, they then will find their true mate, who also is balanced. This is when love and harmony will be both within and outside of oneself. Otherwise, the turmoil within will reflect the experiences going on outside of the individual.

Before I recognized the child within, my path to the light was very laborious and slow. The child within is the truth of our love, living within the heart's emotional body. So it does affect our capacity for receiving and giving love. Our judgment is usually what shuts down our emotional body, creating unwanted feelings and separation. This will also affect the physical body in various ways, creating disease and illness—a person vibrating in their joy is usually healthy and free of disease.

All you have to do is observe a happy little child, full of love and light—joyously creating each moment, secure within the love of a united, happy family. Now see the other side of the coin—the lost, confused, unhappy little child experiencing brutality and separation within the family unit, and you can then have a better picture of what I am saying.

Why do we sometimes choose such a non-functional physical family to come into? Mostly because we need to see that reflection. This will then enable us, sooner or later, to become aware that it is only a reflection, showing us that we need to go within and balance ourselves. Make no mistake about it, we are very powerful Beings, and none of us are victims.

Judgment, if not handled, also causes physical illness and pain, and may be carried from one lifetime to another. Thus something that may have happened in this or an earlier lifetime may then manifest again, in order for us to view it with Love instead of judgment.

This became quite apparent to me in 1993, after moving to Paonia. I was having a lot of pain throughout my body. It was becoming what one might call chronic. I would rise above it during the day by going and spending a lot of my time on a high mountain. One can, if they choose, rise above pain—at least for a while. It is kind of like mind over matter.

However, when alone in the darkness of night, the pain would really return. I had seen chiropractors, and also had acupuncture, which had given me some relief in the past. This time I was really getting the message that I had to heal myself.

This message came in the form of a poem as I lay there. My body really was hurting/aching in many places, especially in the groin of my right leg. I remembered having problems with it before. In fact, while in Santa Fe, there were times when I could barely walk. Acupuncture assisted me greatly and I thought I had cured the problem.

But here it was, knocking at my door again, along with the rest of my body. I knew that nothing in the medical field could help me, except to give me painkillers, which I refuse to take.

So I started asking my Higher Source what I was to do to release this almost crippling pain. This is what I received:

Where do you run when there's no place to run to
Where do you go when there's no place to hide
Who do you turn to when you're lost and alone
You've sunk in the mire and they throw you a stone

Look for the Light, therein lies your answer
Deep down within you, the beginning, the end
God placed that Light there, your blueprint to follow
Be your own teacher, be your own friend

For the Light is your strength, your joy and your passion
The Dark is your teacher, it teaches you well
Once you have learned, thank the Dark for its lesson
Then release it with Love to Heaven, not Hell

Now feel the Joy rising within you,
Expanding, exploding into the Light
No longer earth-bound, your chains have been severed
Come, let us dance in God's beautiful Light

With this message, I had my answer. I was to go within and heal myself, which I proceeded to do. Gently I began touching the area, which was crying out for attention and release, telling it I loved it, pain and all. This is when a picture of a past life started unfolding before me.

I had often gotten a brief glimpse of a ballerina doing a fantastic leap, and then the picture would vanish as fast as it had appeared.

Now, as I breathed love, touching wherever the pain was, the picture started again. However, it didn't fade away. Fascinated, I watched as it unfolded.

I was in Russia. Beautiful music was playing and I was in the spotlight of a scene-filled stage. The auditorium was filled to capacity. A sort of hush was all around me as I gracefully pirouetted across the stage. I could see my black hair, beautiful white skin and lithe torso with the long legs of a dancer.

Then, with what was to be my finale, I leaped high in the air and, in doing so, ended a crumpled heap on the floor, my right leg twisted horribly in back of me.

The audience gasped in disbelief. Instead of applause and numerous curtain calls, I was taken to what appeared to be a medical center. I'm not certain, but feel that my leg was amputated at that time. That would account for the feeling of having had a knife cutting into that groin, which I had felt since the pain started this lifetime.

Of course, this ended my beautiful, pampered career as the leading Ballerina of the Russian Ballet.

So I continued healing my body, touching, sending love to wherever the pain was. It would move from one part of my body to another. This was when I learned what was meant by "turning pain to joy." Now, instead of resisting and judging the pain, I love it, and the pain vanishes. We create and enhance our own pain through resistance.

This has been such a wonderful lesson for me, and also a higher awareness that Love is the key to all things. Once we locate the scenario creating the pain, and remove all judgment, loving that scenario as well as the pain or illness, then the healing really takes place. Pain turns to joy, and we become Masters over our own reality.

I also received the message that, had I not handled that scenario, I would have developed crippling arthritis. Yes, the past does have a direct connection to our present lifetime. This I have proven to myself more than once.

When those haunting memories are brought to the surface, and turned to light by removing all judgment, then magical things occur within the reality of the individual. I know, for I am one of those individuals.

Another episode of a long-forgotten judgment recently came to the fore in my awareness. It was linking my present to a past scenario, where I not only relived my own death, but was able to review how I had been killing people for a false religion—believing that I was serving the Light. That anger, pain and judgment had never been released and so would reflect to me in unexpected ways.

A few weeks prior to my going back and reliving that incident, a friend and I went to Denver. Our mission was to join and assist a group who were meeting with state officials to try to talk them out of dumping truck loads of highly contaminated, radiated waste material over on our side of the mountains. It had been "treated," but was still dangerous.

We had spent the whole day in meetings, showing how dangerous it would be to try to ship such materials over narrow, winding mountain roads. This we succeeded in doing, and they decided to look elsewhere to dump their contamination.

So, happy in the fact that our area was saved from all of that contamination, the next morning we headed back home. A heavy winter storm had been forecast for the higher elevations, which we had to go over in order to get home.

I was driving her Jeep Cherokee and was nearing the top of the pass. We were in the left lane, on our side of the road, going up. A huge cement barrier was between us and the lanes going down.

The left lane, which I was in, was fairly clear and felt safer to me than did the right one. Some cars, a few car lengths behind, were carefully making their way in the right lane as were other cars behind me in the left lane.

We were nearing the top of the pass when my friend insisted that I had to get over into the right lane to let others pass. All of us were going at a sensible rate of speed and, as I said, I felt safe in the lane I was in.

However, she kept insisting and, going against my own better judgment, I tried to cross over into the right lane. Ice and snow lay between the two lanes.

We spun and now were sliding downhill toward the oncoming cars in the left lane. I felt very calm and heard a voice say, "Turn the wheels the way the car is sliding and give it a little more gas." This I did and we slid out of the way of the oncoming cars, crashing against the cement blocks. Somehow I knew that this voice was one of my angel guides.

The Jeep was totaled. My friend and I seemed to be okay, and I still felt very calm. I'm certain whoever was giving me the message, kept me from panicking. Thus we avoided hitting other cars—it could have been quite a pile-up with many injuries, had we met head-on with those coming up.

After being examined by the paramedics, we were on our way home in a tow truck. The pain from where the seat belt restrained me didn't show up until later.

I was wearing a crystal cross pendant and had it under the seat belt instead of over it. It really bruised my breastbone. It was weeks before the pain left and was, at times, excruciating.

It's really remarkable how things happen in order to bring up our "stuff "to be released. While packing, I couldn't find my crystal cross, and I refused to leave without it. So I searched the room, and had the ones staying with me to search their belongings too. The crystal finally appeared in my suitcase, hidden way underneath. Happy to find it, I put it on. Had I not found it until I got home, I never would have experienced the following, which led me to uncovering another long forgotten traumatic core issue.

I kept saying that the pain felt just like a knife piercing me. Suddenly I became aware that I had never been stabbed by a knife or sword this lifetime. So I asked myself how did I know what being stabbed would feel like.

This sent me on an excursion to another scenario, which happened long ago, where judgment, anger, pain and death had stuck me. This is the way judgment of a real heavy past scenario, known as the core issue, will come to the surface through a similar, but less traumatic incident. The lesser incidents will, if allowed, bring the core issues into our conscious mind, so we can release them. Otherwise, we will continue creating incidents of lesser impact until we do.

This core issue was my death back then, and the judgments I placed upon it. Once we discover the core issue of why we keep going around in circles, we can release it. Then, replacing the judgments with love, we stop creating harmful and hurtful scenarios, and are able to rise above the Illusion.

Upon seeing the real reason behind why we continue creating accidents, illness, or any negative scenario, which doesn't appear to be enhancing our present life, we then stop creating from those past influences. In other words, the dark clouds of judgment waiting to be released no longer are around. Then the sunshine of our new awareness lights the way, allowing us to create happier and far more enjoyable times.

Calling in my Guides, Angels, Masters, I asked for the Akashic Records to be opened and to take me back to that core issue.

It wasn't very long until the scene began to unfold. First, I saw myself as a knight in full armor, on a beautiful black horse; he had his protective armor on, too. We were in a bloody battle. I then was told it was during the Crusades.

Suddenly I was lying on the ground, mortally wounded. A lance or staff had pierced my breastbone. I could see my horse's big legs as he stood over me, trying to protect me. I could feel his sadness, his pain, more than my own. I knew that he knew I was dying.

I then felt a burning anger, for I saw how senseless all of this was. There was a deep hatred for a god who would create such a scenario of killing and maiming. I was also very angry at myself for adhering to such a false doctrine of man-made religious beliefs. All this was being made crystal clear.

I saw the Truth and the Light of The Great I AM—the God of Love, not the false warring god of the Illusion. I then saw myself leaving my body. The last scene that was shown to me was my body being placed over the back of my horse, and taken away.

After seeing that scenario in its entirety, and releasing any and all judgment, I replaced it with thankful, loving knowingness that I no longer have to worship the false god of illusion. I am now walking in the Light of the True and Magnificent God of Love. The pain in my chest diminished considerably and soon was no more.

So, whenever haunting memories come knocking at your door, welcome them with an open and loving heart. Heal the wounds of the past, and let the sunshine of awareness light your path with love and gratitude into the wonderful moment of now.

LIFE IS A DANCE

MAKE IT A JOYOUS ONE

AND

WHEN SPIRIT CALLS

GO

If you don't, you will never
know what wondrous gifts might
be awaiting you

MOTHER MEERA—THE AVATAR

I had never searched for Mother Meera. In fact, I was not even aware that she existed. Then, one day, upon opening an Eagle's Path newsletter, staring up at me were the most hypnotic eyes I have ever looked into. For me it was like looking into the eyes of God.

At first, only the eyes were what I was aware of. Finally, my attention was drawn to the rest of the picture and a beautiful face, strong yet feminine, came into view.

There was such a magnetic essence about Her that I had to know more. So, after reading the article, I went to a bookstore and purchased Her book, Answers.

The more I read and gazed into those eyes, the more I wanted to be with Her. This strong of a feeling had never happened to me before. There has, at times, been the urge to go to different seminars, but this feeling was very different—more compelling. Even Bashar never beckoned to me the way She did.

There was such a connection to Her that I could hear Her calling over and over again, "Come to me, child—come to me." That was sometime in July, and I silently made a commitment to go to Germany to see Her.

"This is absurd," part of me said. "There's no money. You don't know a word of German. You'll be all alone in a foreign country. Come on, gal, get real." However, a stronger voice said, "TRUST!" So I did.

My passport was current, so that was a start, and, for some magical reason, money began to appear. Soon I had saved enough to buy my plane ticket and pay for my expenses while there.

My next step was to call the number given in the back of the book and make an appointment. This I did. The date given to me was the following January, which was the anniversary of my son's death.

During that waiting period before going, I could feel Her loving presence all around, guiding and directing me. January finally arrived. It was time to pack my bags and head for Denver, where I was to board the plane that would take me to Germany and Mother Meera.

Here I am, in the middle of winter, driving over high mountain passes which were snow-packed and icy. I hit a blinding snowstorm going over Vale Pass, but there was no feeling of concern or fear.

It was as though I were being carried in the protective arms of Mother God Herself. Since Mother Meera is an Avatar, direct from the essence of Mother God, this did not surprise me in the least.

I had never had much contact with that essence until Mother Meera. It was the Father God essence with whom I was more familiar. In fact, even though there had been opportunities along the way to acquaint myself with that concept, I really hadn't paid very much attention to it until reading Answers.

However, after looking into those eyes, I had no trouble embracing that beautiful, loving concept of God being feminine also. In fact, she became as real, if not more so, as the Father image.

The trip was, for me, wonderful. Even though I couldn't speak a word of German, those whom I choose to call Angels appeared, seemingly out of nowhere, whenever needed.

The first time this happened was when I arrived at the huge train station in Frankfort. I had taken a taxi from the airport instead of the shuttle.

Here I am, stranded in the middle of this humongous station.

Everyone bustling about, in a hurry to catch their train, and I didn't have a clue where to go to get my ticket for Limburg. However, upon asking, a passerby pointed to an information stand ahead of me.

They, in turn, pointed in the direction of a ticket counter, so I proceeded toward it, dragging my one very large suitcase on wheels and carrying another one draped over my shoulder.

I made it to the line and waited for my turn to purchase my ticket. I was having a lot of trepidation as to whether or not the ticket agent would be able to understand me. I didn't speak German and knew nothing about Germany currency.

That was my first encounter with one of my "angels." A tall young man just in front of me asked in perfect English, "Would you like some assistance in purchasing your ticket?" Flabbergasted and relieved at having the good luck of connecting with someone who spoke English, I quickly responded, "Oh, thank you, I'm going to Limburg."

I gave him the amount of money he asked for and he handed me the ticket and some change. Then, picking up my heavy suitcase, he said, "Follow me." So I did, my short legs doing double time, trying to keep up with his long strides. I almost had to run, but was happy to do so. "Here's the train that will take you to Limburg," he told me, handing me back my large case. Then, before I could even thank him, he had disappeared in the crowd.

I don't know whether it was to catch his own train or to help another confused traveler, or maybe both. He may not have been an angel with wings, but he certainly appeared that way to me.

The trip to Limburg was quite enjoyable. The countryside was green, which surprised me because in the dead of winter I expected it to be drab and bleak. Everything seemed to be kept immaculately clean, far different than our country.

When I arrived in Limburg, I could feel Her essence so very strongly—it seemed to be everywhere. I felt like levitating to my Bed and Breakfast some 35 miles away, but opted not to. I was not alone in feeling Her high energy, for others were also remarking about it. Everyone seemed to be in very high spirits, almost like they were being bathed in that energy.

I called the B&B and they said it would be a couple of hours before they could pick me up, and for me to meet them there at the station. This was okay by me, for I was very hungry. The better part of the day had gone by with only a sweet roll and a cup of coffee to sustain me, which I had eaten on the plane before landing in Frankfort.

I asked directions to a restaurant and again was given general information. So here I am, walking down the cobblestone street with my suitcase bumping merrily along behind me

Nothing that came into view had the slightest resemblance to a restaurant, in my estimation. The place that I thought was a restaurant turned out to be a clothing store, so I continued on, doggedly. By then my tummy was really demanding some food. There just wasn't anything indicating that a restaurant was there—of course that was due to the fact that all the signs were in German.

After walking three or four blocks, I retraced my steps. There was a group of teen-age boys and girls congregated at what appeared to be a sort of a resting area with benches in the middle of the street.

Walking up to them, I asked if any of them spoke English. Several did, so I told them I wanted to find some place that served food. One young man came over, and grabbing my suitcase off he went, with me right on his heels.

He took me back to the store that I had thought was a restaurant, and told me to go downstairs. Then he went racing back to join his friends. I shouted, "thank you" after him. Another Angel—who knows?

There was a display case with all kinds of food. Picking out something that looked good, I handed the girl behind the counter a fist full of German coins. She gave me back a good deal of change, and I sat down to enjoy my first German food. She could have kept all of the money, and I never would have known the difference.

It was getting almost time for me to meet up with my ride, so after eating I picked up my luggage and headed back to the train station.

The man who picked me up was the owner of the B&B I was to stay at. He seated me in the front seat of his BMW, and I buckled my seatbelt and experienced how the Germans drive—wild and fast. They all seem to drive like there is no tomorrow and the devil is right on their heels.

Arriving at the B&B, I went to my room to unpack, and was

almost bowled over by Her powerful energy. It seemed to be everywhere. I arrived at my destination on Thursday and was to attend my first Darshan on Friday night. I was scheduled again for Saturday, Sunday and Monday, and would return home on the following Tuesday.

Settling in for the night, I noticed that there was no feeling of being tired, just a peaceful, happy one. Waking up early the next morning, I dressed and went down to breakfast. I was very hungry, and was ready for what I thought a German breakfast would be.

Boy, was I wrong, instead of sausage, eggs and potatoes, it consisted of juice, cold hard-boiled eggs, cold cuts, cold cereal, hard rolls, butter, jam and coffee. A little disappointed, I ate it anyway. This was to be my breakfast every morning for the duration of my stay at the B&B.

I was too happy to let anything like food dampen my spirits. It was Friday and tonight I would be seeing Mother Meera for the first time. I didn't know what to expect, but felt that what I was about to experience would be great. I wasn't wrong; in fact, it was awesome.

As per schedule, the group of us that were staying at the same B&B met and was taken by car to the little town of Dornburg-Thalheim, which is the home of Mother Meera.

Around 300 people had traveled from all over the world to experience and be in Her energy. We all gathered in her large home, where she conducted her Darshans.

Before going in, we were instructed to be very quiet. We were told where to sit by Adilskshmi, Mother Meera's secretary, devotee and, as near as I could tell, a sort of protector, watching over The Mother like a Guardian Angel.

All of us were seated, quietly awaiting the moment for Her to enter the room. In fact, the room was so quiet, you could have heard a pin drop. Suddenly, as one, we all stood. Evidently we had all felt Her presence entering the room, for there had been no signal, at least to my knowledge.

Then this beautiful Being swept into the room, permeating it with Her essence. My emotions were so high that I could feel my heart pounding. She was, to say the least, awe-inspiring.

The first night I had the privilege of having a seat very close to Mother Meera. It was fascinating to watch as She received each individual. One at a time they would come to Her and would kneel down to receive their Darshan. All 300 of us took our turn when we each felt we were ready, as instructed.

Seating Herself, the Darshans began. As each person knelt in front of Her, She would then place Her hands on the head. Her eyes were closed. Then, removing Her hands, She would open Her eyes and look deep into the eyes of that person. Then, once again, Her eyes would close and the Darshan was over and he/she would return to their seat.

I felt it was time for me to go up to receive mine. So I proceeded to the "waiting chair" and waited for Her to finish the Darshan She was giving. While sitting there, I found myself wondering how I was going to kneel, trying to orchestrate the scenario.

However, I didn't have long to wait, for suddenly I found myself in front of Her and kneeling, my head going so far down, it was almost touching Her feet. I felt Her hands touching my head and a tingle of high energy ran all the way down my spine.

As She removed Her hands, I leaned back and saw Her eyelids starting to open. Her long eyelashes were like curtains parting. As I looked into Her eyes, I felt I was becoming a part of Her and She me, and found myself spinning into other worlds, other dimensions.

Then I became aware that once again the curtains were being drawn as Her eyelids closed. My Darshan was over. I floated more than walked back to my chair.

Every night the Darshans were the same, but the feelings were different. The second night I was placed farther back and over to the side, where I could only catch glimpses of Her. After my Darshan, which again was awesome, I returned to my seat, but for some reason was feeling abandoned and separated from Her.

Just as I became aware of how I was feeling, I also became aware that Lord Jesus was standing beside me. He was surrounded in a golden cloud of energy with His white robe swirling around His feet.

He stayed with me until the Darshans had ended. I didn't feel abandoned any longer. Instead, I felt engulfed in the warmth of His love. He disappeared just as we all got to our feet, as The Mother swept out of the room. What an experience that was—Mother Meera and Lord Jesus, both in the same night.

The next two nights were also different. On the third night, my whole body was trembling with very high energy. On the fourth and final night, there was so much love that I could feel myself crying from sheer ecstasy.

Then, it was Tuesday and time to return home. The old "Grand Dame," which I called her—she was the mother of the owner of the B&B—was a trip, to say the least. She never said a word except once in a while, "nein," or something like that, with a disapproving stare.

She would do this if, while eating breakfast, one of us didn't put our egg shells in the proper container, or if we made some other kind of faux pas which she didn't approve of. Then out would come her finger, shaking vigorously and pointing to the right container while saying "nein." She appeared to be quite stern.

However, Tuesday morning she was down in the dining room bright and early to see that I had some breakfast before taking the taxi to the station. As the taxi driver loaded my suitcases, she and I stood there looking at each other. I didn't know what to say and evidently she didn't either. Then, remembering the words "Auf Wiedersehn," which, I believe, means *God Be With You*. I said it to her.

Grabbing my hands and shaking them up and down, her face broke into a beautiful smile as she repeated "Auf Wiedersehn" over and over again. We had broken the language barrier, which also broke her stern, silent veneer. She wasn't the holy terror she appeared to be, but a beautiful, warm person.

Climbing into the taxi, I waved goodbye to her as we drove off. We arrived at the train station in Limburg. Once again I was wondering what train to catch. There were several tracks from which to choose.

Nervously I asked a girl sitting next to me if she spoke English. She didn't. Suddenly, another "angel" appeared, this time in the guise of a blond woman.

"Are you going to the airport in Frankfort?" she asked in perfect English.

Again relief swept over me as I answered, "yes." Just then a train pulled into the station.

"This is ours," she said, picking up my heavy piece of luggage. So off we went, boarded the train and seated ourselves. We had a lovely visit during the ride to Frankfort.

Her home had been Germany, but she now resided in Canada. She was visiting her family and was meeting some friends for a day on the town in Frankfort.

Some distance out of Frankfort, she said, "I'll have to keep a close watch, for it won't be long until we change trains. It can get quite tricky if you don't know when to get off. This is it," she told me, picking up my heavy case again.

So we got off of one train and back on another, which took us directly to the airport. She then took me to where I was to board my plane, handed me back my luggage, saying, "I've got to run. Have a nice trip home," and off she went, disappearing into the crowd.

I've often thought that if she hadn't come along and assisted me, I might still be riding that train—a lost soul traveling from station to station, never knowing when or where to get off—now that's a scary thought.

However, angels do appear when needed. They have for me more than once. Synchronicity always amazes me.

What are the odds that a traveler from the U.S. meets someone from Canada in a train station in Germany, in order to be guided to the right train that will take her to the right area where her plane is embarking? Ah, Mother Meera, you really were looking after me, weren't you?

I boarded my plane and was on my way back home, full of love, light and high energy. That afternoon we were scheduled to watch the show Forrest Gump, which I was looking forward to seeing with great anticipation. However, that was not to be.

We were just getting into it when I got this message: "Look outside." The shades had all been pulled for the movie. Upon asking the flight attendant, she directed me to a rear seat where the light from the window would not affect the screen. Opening the shade, I beheld an unforgettable sight.

There before my eyes was a glorious golden river with what appeared to be waves of burnished gold rippling through it. I sat there for a long time just drinking in its beauty. Then I received this message: "This is God's Golden River of Unconditional Love."

What a thrilling gift and such a beautiful sight. I will never forget that moment nor cease to be grateful. Needless to say, I did not feel cheated for having missed the movie.

When Spirit calls, go. You'll never know, if you don't, what wondrous gifts might be awaiting you.

For almost three years after my visit to Mother Meera, I could feel Her wonderful essence around me—healing, guiding me with Her Unconditional Love. I was so very happy and in tune with life.

During that time, whenever I had a pain or felt ill, all I had to do was call on Her and ask it to be removed. It would disappear as if by magic. The Awakenings were becoming more powerful and my energy and awareness had taken a giant leap.

The love I felt from and for Her was beautiful. In other words, there was a connection that distance and time had no effect on.

Then, gradually I became aware that I was no longer feeling that high energy. Someway, somehow, I had become separated from Her beautiful essence and I was missing it. "It must be me," I thought, and so I decided to make the journey one more time, in order to reconnect with Her.

When or how I was going to do it, I wasn't certain. I had to get a new passport; my old one had expired. My money inflow was rather sparse. Since I no longer was connected to Her energy, everything seemed to be slowing down.

I went to Grand Junction and got my passport. "At least that's a start," I told myself. However, still there was no real enthusiasm on my part, nor was the money flowing in like it had done before.

Finally, I called and made my appointment for the following January, three years from the date of my last visit.

There was also some trepidation about going. Was I being told not to go, I wondered? However, I was determined to reconnect with that beautiful energy again, so by-passed those feelings.

Everything seemed to be in place, except that high enthusiasm. "What's wrong? Why am I feeling this way? I should be elated, for soon I will be kneeling in front of my beloved Mother Meera," I told myself.

There was no fear, only a sort of "Well, I'm going to Germany. So what?"

I knew that I would have my answers as to why the rift between us when I knelt in front of Her again. However, I certainly was not prepared for the scenario I was about to encounter.

your job is to hold the Light!

do not try to be a savior for there are no
victims thus no one needs to be saved
for each must walk his own path
into understanding and unconditional
love in his own time.

you may, however, assist when asked

WALKING OUT OF THE ILLUSION

Stepping off of the train in Limburg, almost three years to the day after my first journey, eagerly I searched for Her beautiful essence. Somewhat surprised at feeling nothing except the different vibrations that make up the third density world, I brushed it off with "Oh well, I'm probably tired," which was true. However, the high energy that had sent me soaring before was not there.

Oh sure, there still were those wonderful Angels—people assisting me whenever it was needed, such as information. However, the essence for which I had made this journey was nowhere to be felt. It was as though She no longer was on the planet.

"Well," I told myself, "when I get to my room at the Bed and Breakfast, I'll feel Her beautiful high energy and everything will be wonderful again."

Not so, for upon arriving at my room in the same B&B I had stayed at before, there was only the low, third-dimensional vibration waiting to greet me. The light, the uplifting energy that had sent me soaring was nowhere around there either.

Settling in for the night, I unpacked. The owners remembered me and it was a nice, friendly feeling to have them around. At least, there still was some familiarity, which was a poor substitute for Her beautiful energy.

I awoke late Friday morning, tired, almost missing breakfast. The trip, the jet lag and time difference, which had not affected me before, was very apparent this time. Without Her high energy, everything seemed to be different and rather heavy.

Somewhat surprised at having overslept and knowing that I might not be served breakfast, I jumped up, hastily dressed, and ran downstairs.

They graciously served me some breakfast, even though it was almost noon. Once again I checked to see if Her energy was around, and again felt disappointment. It just wasn't there.

"Tonight," I thought, "I will be at the Darshan and all will be as it was before." I couldn't have been more wrong. When She walked into the room, I put my hand over my heart and asked for it to open. Having done this many times on my own, it was no surprise that it did. However, for some reason there seemed to be lacking that intense energy which was so prevalent before.

I watched as, one by one, they went to Her, kneeling. Yes, the Darshans were the same. However, the high electrifying energy seemed to be missing. "Something's wrong," I kept thinking. "Maybe I'll get that feeling back when I go up." Then it was my turn, so I went up and knelt in front of Her.

Her hands reached out, touching my head. I felt nothing. I looked into Her eyes and was aware that they no longer were the eyes of Mother God but those of another mortal. They were beautiful, but the power, the fire, the passion was not there. They didn't send me spinning off into other worlds as before. I also noticed that the Darshan had been shortened, noticeably. It was over almost as soon as it had begun, and I didn't "float" back to my chair as I had done after receiving my first Darshan three years earlier.

I felt bewildered and, yes, somehow betrayed. My thoughts were darting here and there, trying to figure out why I wasn't feeling the way I had at our first encounter. However, others at the B&B were saying that they, too, felt nothing—zippo. Some even went so far as to say that "yes, She was beautiful, but that She was not the great Avitar she claimed to be." It was not at all like the comments the time before.

I knew from my last trip that there was a power so magnificent, so wonderful within Mother Meera, that I and everyone else experienced miraculous changes, both within our bodies and our lives.

Saturday night was the same. Around 200 people were there receiving Darshan. Still I felt nothing. Sunday I spent most of the day working with the energies, sending Mother Meera love and light, telepathically asking Her why the change of energy.

I received a message that something or someone was blocking Her energy. "Was it being blocked only from me or from others, and who or what was blocking it?" No answer. So I continued sending her my love and light, hoping for some kind of a connection.

Darshan that night was the same. It was, for me, as though She were going through the motions without the high vibration of the Avatar.

Monday night was no different as far as feeling anything during the Darshan. As She left the room it was apparent to me, that the powerful energy, which was so predominant before, was no longer with her. "Is this part of the Illusion, or is this for real?" I asked—still no answer.

I felt compassion and empathy for this beautiful Being, as I recalled that strong and vibrant essence that illuminated the room as she swept into it three years ago. Now Her body seemed frail, vulnerable. She appeared to be rather bent over as She walked—a mere shadow of the powerful Being that I had experienced on my last visit.

I also noticed that Adilskshmi was no longer around. Could this be the problem? Upon asking of her whereabouts, someone said she had returned to India for a vacation. Was it a permanent split? This I never found out.

I watched as others knelt by Her chair, from which she administered the Darshans. They seemed to be worshipping that empty chair, as though they were drinking in an energy that I could no longer feel.

"Perhaps," I thought, "if I went and knelt down, I could feel what they were feeling." And that was the moment I walked out of the Illusion.

ARDA GOLDEN EAGLE WOMAN

The Vision

As I stood there, contemplating whether or not to join the others who were kneeling at Her chair, there seemed to be a shift in my reality. Instead of seeing a few people kneeling, there were thousands. All of them kneeling, asking for forgiveness, for strength, or for whatever they felt they lacked within themselves. Some were kneeling before other mortals, others before crosses or other religious objects.

I saw where this had been, and still was happening all over the planet. All were asking to be raised out of their guilt, their pain, somehow feeling that they were victims, and someone else had the power to release them from what they had created.

I watched, fascinated, and knew beyond a shadow of a doubt that I no longer was a part of that illusion. "How can I help them to realize who they truly are? To bring forth the knowingness that they and only they are responsible for creating and buying into their own victimhood?" I silently asked.

Then the message came to me, clear and simple: *You cannot, for each must walk his own path into understanding and unconditional love. The Tree of Life is for everyone and each must partake of it in his/her own way and in his/her own time. That is the God Given Free Will of everyone. Do not try to be a savior, for no one is a victim, thus no one need be saved. However, you may assist when asked, and only then. Be a channel for The Light of Truth and Love Unconditionally.*

Then the vision left, my eyes cleared, seeing only the few dozen kneeling. I put my coat on and walked out the door, feeling somehow free, unattached, very powerful, and yet at the same time very humble and grateful. And, just maybe, a little lost.

The next day my body started chilling, mucus was running out of my nose and mouth. I was alone in the B&B, for all the other guests had gone home. I had arranged to stay for the next four Darshans.

All day Wednesday I stayed in bed, not eating, only drinking water. That night my body started a series of releasing through vomiting, which continued most of the night.

I felt that, although it was like a flu, my body was releasing things which no longer served it. Each time I threw up there was a feeling of more and more power coming into me. It was as though I wasn't in my body, but watching it from a distance.

There was no feeling of fear, even though I was completely alone in a strange country whose language I couldn't speak. The owners had gone home for the night, for they lived in homes separate from the B&B. There was, however, a knowingness that I was walking through the illusion of body illness and so placed no judgment upon it.

Somewhere around dawn, the clearing or releasing came to an end. "I need more Light," I said. "Please send me an angel," and went to sleep.

Staying in my room all day Thursday and Thursday night, I began questioning the validity of a god whose power seemed to be focused more on the negative than the positive energies. Why were there so much pain, hate, greed, judgment, disappointment, and war? Was this the true God leading us down a path of empty promises and unfulfilled dreams, lifetime after lifetime, or had we in some way been duped?

I'm sure that most of us have had these kinds of disturbing thoughts at one time or another. Thus we try desperately to find an answer that would somehow stop our senseless gyration, placing us on a direct path out of the Illusion.

Oh yes, we have prayed to God for deliverance and, when there was no deliverance, we either became embittered and gave up, or took the bull by the horns and pulled ourselves out of our dilemma. If we did the latter, we probably did learn to be more careful as to what we created—experience is a great teacher.

I had experienced and learned so much, for which I was very thankful. However, I still had this burning question: Was all that I had been told, taught and given as "gospel truth" really the Great I AM's Word, or had a controlling force taken over? Was it somehow blocking our memories of who we were, and our connection to The Most High God of Unconditional Love and Light?

Remembering my death back during the Crusades, once again I felt my anger and frustration of having served a god of war, hate and destruction, using us as instruments to kill and maim, all in the name of love.

It all seemed so "crystal clear" then. However, upon leaving my body, I evidently was once again caught in the web of Illusion's forgetfulness, and so returned again and again to replay lifetimes of not knowing who I was.

It wasn't until recently that I was able to break those chains that kept me in my fog of forgetfulness. This happened when I rose above Earth's Illusion and allowed myself to come out of my judgments and fear. Thus I no longer have to walk in those dark shadows.

The Bible's Old Testament stated clearly, "I am a jealous and vengeful god," emphasizing judgment and punishment. These words seemed to be threatening those who did not adhere to "the laws of God" with eternal damnation, and forever burning in hell's fire. We have also been told to "separate the wheat from the chaff." Perhaps that was some kind of warning from the real loving God or one of Its messengers.

How many people, through their religious beliefs, are free of control? Are they really free, or are they afraid to stray from "the path of righteousness" for fear of punishment?

Was this truly what The Great I AM—Father/Mother God—ask of Their beloved children? If we, as the reflection of God, want only the best for our children, then wouldn't it stand to reason They would want the same for us? And why Free Will, if we were to be punished for not adhering to abstaining from partaking of the glorious banquet that supposedly has been given to us? Is this really free will?

"Where did all of this crap come from?" I asked myself. Evidently the Truth of The Written Word has been changed considerably from what God intended.

The more I questioned, the more I realized that something was very fishy about Earth's whole setup. I have vivid memories of being thrown into a dungeon for taking a stand against the changing of God's Word.

Selacia hit upon this during a session with The Council of Twelve. I already knew I had died there, but never said a word about that incident to her. She, through going back to that time with The Council of Twelve in order to erase the judgments and memories, confirmed that which I already knew.

So that core issue is no more. I no longer feel I have to escape. This has been an issue of mine all this lifetime, until They went back and released it, replacing it with the knowingness that I am always free. No longer do I have the feeling of having to escape from anything.

I have fond memories of being in Lemuria during its evolvement. There never seemed to be any controls or heaviness at that time. We were free to explore, create, and enjoy to our heart's content with no thought of fear or punishment. Fear was not within our understanding, nor was jealousy or hate. It was a Garden of Eden, where all was love and joy. We were, at that time, the joyful laughter of the child.

Then, just before the fall of Lemuria, there was a great shift in energies. The Lightness of Being became more solid, heavier. We, who had been so free—able to come and go off of the planet at will—were finding it more and more difficult to even levitate, let alone leave.

As time went by, the atmosphere became more dense, more suppressive. Who or what was casting a controlling negative spell? Was it really The Great I AM, or some lesser entity setting himself up as God, creating this illusion, thus creating a prison planet? Did we become the pawns of this lesser god, while the love and the light of the true God were being shut down within our consciousness? And was the story of the Snake and Adam and Eve, a direct reflection of what was taking place?,

All I know was that as time went by, the Love of God gradually became more of a myth, a story handed down from generation to generation, without much of the real energy of love reflected in Earth's children.

As the Ego Mind set itself up as supreme ruler of Earth, Lemuria sank into its watery grave of forgetfulness, taking the joyous laughter of the child with It.

Atlantis then made its grand entrance with a dazzling display of what the mind can do when filled with knowledge, and led by Ego, without the love of the heart. This is still being reflected today all over the planet.

Then as the false god gained more and more control, Atlantis rose to greater heights of power, and eventually destroyed Itself through Ego.

However, since there must be a balance in all things, the great and glorious GOD I AM is once again reflecting Its Light of Truth upon Earth. The Masters and Angels are also appearing to us, bringing forth and revealing The Divine Plan. This is bringing us to a higher understanding, and loosening the grasp of the false god's control and judgment.

The Love and Light that was Lemuria, once again is rising up, reflecting the true love of the Great I AM. While the Illusion with its fear, judgment, hate, and death is now slowly sinking under the waves of forgetfulness, never to rise again.

Upon asking what could I do to be of assistance in these troubled and traumatic times, I was told: The most important thing for all of you to remember is to hold the Light and release all judgment. *The divine plan is unfolding as decreed.*

Is what I was shown truth or fiction, or somewhere in between? This I don't know. I only knew what was shown to me was, for me, very real. I finally fell into a deep, peaceful sleep.

Waking up Friday morning and sensing a shift in energy, I dressed and went downstairs to the dining room. Wonder of wonders, not only had I been granted one angel, but a whole minibus of them in the form of Reiki Masters from England.

They brought a lot of light with them and they spoke English, although some of it I could barely understand—there were so many dialects spoken just among those fourteen Light Messengers.

I jokingly offered to teach them true English, but for some reason they laughingly declined. They were a great bunch with whom I could communicate, giving and receiving love.

Several of them also became quite ill during their three-day stay. My knowingness told me that they, too, were no longer under the protective energy of Mother Meera.

On one of my trips into Limburg, I visited a little crystal shop. The owner apparently spoke no English and I no German, but that did not stop us from having a wonderful heart connection. I kept feeling a particular crystal calling to me, but no matter how I tried, I couldn't find it.

He had a very special dog with soulful eye. She would take my hand in her mouth and lead me all around the room, as if assisting me in finding that illusive crystal which was calling so loudly.

Finally, I decided to give up my search for my special crystal. Just as I was leaving, he held up his hand as if to say, "Wait a minute," then, reaching down underneath the shelf that kept calling to me, he pulled out a beautiful piece of carnelian and placed it in my hand as a gift. It was the crystal, which had been calling to me.

I felt the urge to hug him and he me, so we just kept hugging, enjoying each other's energy. Finally, not knowing what to say, I said, "I love you." He answered back in perfect English, "I love you, too."

The connection made, I left, knowing that we will always be connected. All I have to do is pick up that beautiful crystal and his loving energy is with me.

What a wonderful feeling to know that distance, like death, is only an illusion and, as Richard Bach said, *There's no such place as far away.* It is only the illusion that locks us into the concept of separation.

I attended three more Darshans, for I wanted to check out the energies after walking out of the Illusion. Again I felt nothing as far as high energies were concerned. Only a beautiful love for Mother Meera and all that she had done for me.

Thank you, beautiful Lady, for your love and your guidance during those three years that I felt so connected to you. I realize now that the cords had to be severed to enable me to walk out of the Illusion. A Master never hangs onto a student, but instead sets them free when they are ready. And You knew that I was ready.

The plane trip back home was not the same as the one experienced before—no beautiful messages, no uplifting displays. Most of all, that wonderful vibrant energy which I had come to depend on was no longer available for me. It was as if I had suddenly been cut loose from Her support, and I didn't like the feeling.

"Have I really escaped from Illusion's trap?" I wondered. From all indications of my physical body, I seemed to be a heck of a lot worse off than before I embarked on this strange journey to Germany.

My physical body still seemed to be stuck within Illusion's mighty grasp while the rest of me was soaring ever higher. "Am I going to have to give up this earthly body in order for the rest of me to escape Illusion's dark energy?"

I was more than willing to do so, but how? Was I to follow in the footsteps of my son, in order not to lose what I had gained spiritually? There were so many things left unfinished, i.e. Awakenings, my book, Thor still depended on me, the list went on and on.

However, unless I could get my body vibrating in a higher vibration, closer to the rest of me, I knew that I no longer would be able to accomplish that which I knew was a part of my commitment to The Light.

My body was beginning to feel old, no longer vibrant and full of enthusiasm, which was also bringing the rest of me down along with it.

"It's 1999, less than a year before the new Millennium. After that happens, things will be much better." It was MeAmba, my beautiful Higher Soul coming to my rescue. *"There's going to be some rough times coming up for the next few months,"* she told me. *"However, ride them out. You'll be happy you did. For you then will see not only a new millennium, but also a different and more expanded you. Trust, child, trust, and remember I am always with you."*

She then went on to say that the wonderful energy of Mother Meera would be restored within my consciousness, for it is the same divine energy of Mother God and is always available.

She also said that in order for me to be able to walk out of the Mass Conscious Illusion, the withdrawing of Mother Meera's energy was necessary. That was the reason for my second trip to Germany.

The physical body, being much more vulnerable to the lower vibrational energies, is more susceptible to illness. Thus it would continue functioning in less than a desirable state through the year 1999.

However, at the same time, it would become stronger, more vibrant after the beginning of the new millennium. Its vibration would be of a higher, more compatible nature to the rest of my bodies. This all was given to me through MeAmba.

So, like the saying goes, "Fasten your seat belt, it's going to be a bumpy ride." I decided to do just that. I had committed myself to being here for the "Grand Finale," so why give up now?

And yes, it did turn out to be a very bumpy ride.

Enter the sacred temple

of your heart where
Love abides

When you do, all is equal
and
Joy reigns supreme

THE HEART ALWAYS KNOWS

I arrived back home in the State of Separation. The Illusion seemed to really have gotten quite a hold on my physical body. It felt tired, having a difficult time keeping up with the rest of me.

Spiritually, mentally and emotionally I stayed above the fray. However, my physical body was not in such a high vibration. It was itching, and several areas were breaking out.

I scratched, put lotion on, to no avail. It was getting worse and driving me nuts. Something was eating me, and I wasn't sure just what it was. Had I picked up some kind of an incurable disease? Again no answer.

Finally, in desperation, I went to see my all-knowing friend, Dr. Jim. "What's wrong with me, anyway?" I asked as he checked me out.

"Nothing that can't be cured," he assured me. "You've just gotten yourself a good dose of parasites." He then gave me some pills, muscle-tested me for dosage, and sent me home.

Hurrying home, I opened the bottle, got a glass of water, and started to swallow one. It was one big pill, at least for me. It caught in my throat. I drank more water but couldn't get it to budge.

By now I was gasping for air. The water came back up, but the pill didn't. Finally, in desperation—not being able to breathe—I bent way over, doubled up my fist, and pushed with all my might on my stomach. The pill shot out of my mouth, and once again I was breathing.

"Now what in the heck am I going to do? I'm not going through that again," I told myself. So, calling Dr. Jim, I got my answer. "Chew them up and drink lots of water," he told me. This I did—the taste was horrible. However, it did the trick and gradually the itching stopped, the abrasions cleared up, and I was feeling a lot better—all of me.

However, that was short-lived, for on July 1, the Illusion decided I had rested long enough, and I went into agreement.

I had taken Thor to the vet to have some foxtails removed from his ears. They were all over the area where we lived. She said they could be quite dangerous, traveling to the brain, which could result in a very painful death.

Knocking him out, she proceeded to remove them, cleaned his teeth, and did a few other things while he was in "lullaby land." He was still rather out of it when we got home.

It was late, almost suppertime. He wanted to go out. I was tired but slipped into a pair of very light, non-supportive slippers, and went with him over some pretty rough and rocky terrain. He disappeared. Forgetting about me, I quickened my step and went dashing off, not paying any attention to where I was going, calling, "Thor, Thor, come back!"

The toe of my light slipper caught on something, sending me sprawling. I landed with all my weight on my right hand on a very hard and unyielding rock. I remember saying as I went down, "Nothing's going to break," but at the same time I was very fearful that it had.

The breath was knocked out of me, and my right hand and wrist felt sort of numb. I dragged myself to a rock and sat on it, trying to assess the damage. Had I broken any bones? Nothing seemed to be broken, but the pain in my right hand and wrist was excruciating.

I was feeling nauseous and dizzy, but knew I had to make it back to the house a short distance away. "There's no one around to rescue you, so pull yourself together and get moving," I told myself. Again I was on my own and had to deal with my body the best way I could.

Slowly, painfully, I made it back to the house. Thor was waiting for me on the front porch. He always seems to appear after something like this happens.

"You knuckle-head, you could have come back before I fell, then this wouldn't have happened," I scolded. He wagged his stub of a tail, apologetically, and followed me into the house.

"It's not broken, it's not broken," I kept saying over and over again as I applied ice to my wrist and hand. The wrist was swelling some, but I could move all my fingers, which was, for me, a good sign.

Two days later I went to see Dr. Jim. He examined me and didn't believe it was broken. So, painful as it was, I kept on driving, having to shift gears with my poor little hurt right hand, with only an ace bandage to support it.

A month went by. The pain in my wrist was not much better. However, the swelling was almost gone. I kept on driving, going up on the Grand Mesa, where it was cooler and always gave me a lift. This, by now, I needed. However, it wasn't helping my wrist to heal. I was in complete denial as far as a broken wrist was concerned.

It was getting close to the time for me to speak at Ann's Love and Light Conference. No progress was being made on writing my book. My poor little wrist just could not tolerate anything like typing on a word processor.

Now it was time to attend the conference. My wrist was really hurting. However I ignored it, and drove some 70 miles round trip every day to be at the conference for those three days. A couple of well-meaning, very aware healers tried to tell me that my wrist was broken. I would have no part of that, so paid no attention to them.

By the time the conference was over my wrist was really giving me a bad time, so I went to another doctor. He said it was broken in three different places, and had me get a wristband to protect it.

Dr. Jim, who has been and still is so "right on" when he diagnoses me, evidently had "missed the boat" that time. It could have been that I was blocking him with my stubborn determination that it was not broken. I, at that time, probably would not have accepted any other finding.

Fall came and went. By now my hands, both of them, were stiff and rather painful, and to make matters worse my left wrist was also giving me trouble. Evidently I had somehow managed to develop some arthritis in both—double trouble.

I tried to write and got nowhere. Nothing was flowing as far as creativity was concerned. I was doing some Awakenings and quite a lot of channeling and the rest of the time explored the Grand Mesa. This sent my spirit soaring, enabling me to heal my physical body. Soon my wrists were free from pain and back to normal.

I found myself settling into just doing nothing and the creative part of me wasn't too happy about that. I wanted to go places, do things, and be somebody which, in my judgment, just wasn't happening.

"I'm getting nowhere, fast," I told myself. Oh, sure, I had healed my wrists and the pain was gone. However, it was becoming the same old same old—at least that was how I was beginning to look at it. Even the place where we were living was becoming less than desirable. Where it used to thrill me to look out of my window, seeing deer grazing, and awesome sunsets over the Mesa, now it was like "ho-hum, so what?"

I wanted to move, to go somewhere else, but didn't. Then, once again, Universe did some shaking up. My landlord and his wife, who had been trying to sell their home in Grand Junction ever since I had rented their little mobile home, suddenly announced that they had sold it. Since the place I was living in now would be their home, I would have to move.

This happened on December 1 of 1999. I had one month to find a place that would let me have Thor and move. Now it's hard enough to find some place to rent that will take a small pet. However, since Thor is a 110-pound Doberman-Rottweiler, it was beginning to look like an impossibility.

I began packing and looking for something I could afford that would take Thor. I was not about to abandon my old friend, even though he, at times, was a pain in the rear. We had come too far for me to jump ship now.

Finally, after combing the area, including several small towns within a radius of fifty miles or more, and coming up with either they were too expensive or were real "rat traps," I lucked out.

Another angel appeared. Her name was Liz, a German lady, who lived in Cedaredge. I hadn't seen her for some time, and just happened to run into her at the local grocery store.

Upon asking how I was doing, I told her my plight. She knew of a place, in town, a small mobile home, but wasn't certain of the phone number of the one that owned it. She told me it was near her home. So, after a few trips up and down the streets of the little town, there it was—a lovely little place, fenced yard, and with a "for rent" sign.

Jotting the number down, I made an appointment and met up with the new owner, who had just purchased it. He and his wife had wonderful energy, and we connected immediately. They had no problem accepting Thor, once they checked our records from past landlords, which they told me were excellent.

So, signing the contracts, I finished packing. Friends came on moving day and I was all settled in by December 20—the day I had targeted to move.

Suddenly I was feeling better. For some reason the "excitement of the chase," that is to say the move and all, assisted in getting me out of my doldrums. After all, there really was no time for such nonsense, what with packing, moving and with Christmas and Y2K just around the corner.

The new home was adorable. Thor, after three days of moping, and not eating, decided it was okay after all, and became quite happy in his new surroundings.

Y2K passed without a hitch, as I knew it would. I started getting quite a few people who wanted Awakenings. This kept me busy, but still my body was not up to par. It still wasn't soaring with the rest of me.

Evidently I still was not paying attention to what my physical body was telling me. I had been too busy with all that had transpired to do any more than just feed it. It wasn't getting the tender loving care it was crying for, and soon let me know in no uncertain terms, in the form of a very bad cold. Colds are usually an indication of a loss that has been judged and never released. There still remained the feeling of my separation from Mother Meera, which, in itself, was a huge loss.

Coughing and sneezing, all I could think of was making my body feel better. My soaring became a feeble flapping of wings. Once again my body was saying, "I'm here, I'm part of you. Take care of me." It was very apparent to me that I needed to pay attention to it if I wanted to get well.

For six weeks it demanded attention. No longer was I able to go sailing off into the wild blue yonder, dragging it along whether it wanted to go or not. However, since all things must come to an end, whatever I had been experiencing ended with just a few sniffles remaining. I bid it a not-so-fond adieu, happy to be rid of it. Now I could get back to a more normal life, whatever that was.

Good Friday and Easter were approaching and, because of my lowered vibration, once again I found myself remembering that scenario of long ago with its painful, haunting memories.

With each passing day I became more entrapped within the web of my own guilt and judgments. I seemed unable to rise above it, and the Mass Consciousness' dramatization of Jesus on the cross—the lower vibrations on the planet really love to play that scene to the max. Being empathic, I was being caught within those vibes, which was lowering my vibration even more. I wanted to run, but where? One cannot run away or hide from one's self. This I knew.

I tried tuning it out by watching TV sitcoms. However, the advertisement of the forthcoming mini series of the life of Jesus put it right in my face—crucifixion and all.

"Why am I going through this again?" I asked myself. I had received information through channeling, and thought I had cleared myself of any and all repercussions of that long ago scenario—at least that was what my mind kept telling me.

However, my heart knew better. It was telling me that there was a part of me that had not been set free. Thus I was still caught up in the judgments and dramatizations relating to that time.

The time had come to go within and put it to rest, once and for all—no matter what it took. I also knew that it would take a very powerful master to assist me in doing this. Picking up the phone, I called Samuel, a.k.a. Zandrion, and asked him for a session. He agreed and soon I was speeding toward Grand Junction, where he lived.

Samuel greeted me, ushered me into his home, and I took a seat in a very special chair. In front of me were the pictures of the feminine Masters: Mother Mary, Mother Meera, Kuan Yin, as well as Lord Jesus, Archangel Michael and others, all of whom represented the powerful Spirit of Mother/Father God—in Its many forms.

I drew two cards from his Angel deck—both called to me. One was the Angel of Wisdom, the other the Angel of All the Time Awareness, both of which, to me, felt so powerful and so right.

Samuel invoked those energies to come into the circle and the session began. It was a silent session with no talking. However, he did play a CD of inspirational music, working with his powerful crystal pendulum, Zandrion, and Angels.

I felt Mother Mary's beautiful energy, and was aware that she was speaking to me. She was explaining that there had been a blockage placed within my heart at that long ago time—placed there by my own self-judgment and guilt, and which I had carried to this day.

Gently She removed it, and as She did, I could feel my body jerk. Tears were rolling down my cheeks. The blockage within my heart that I had carried with me for so long melted away. With a sigh of relief, I opened my eyes. The energies changed and the session was over. Silently I thanked Mother Mary and the other Masters, Angels, Zandrion.

Mission accomplished, Samuel and I went to lunch, and had a delightful exchange of what was taking place on the planet at that time. I then said goodbye and was on my way back home. The trip was rather vague.

I knew I was not completely in my body, but I also knew that I was protected. It took me almost another day before completely re-entering my physical body. As I said, it was one powerful session.

I also shed a few buckets full of tears that night, which released a tremendous amount of pent-up emotions that I had carried for so long. It felt wonderful, and with the sobs, which were heavy and many, I felt so much lighter, peaceful and grateful, thanking all who had come to my rescue. At last my physical body was more in sync with the rest of me.

I was really feeling great, with lots of energy—ready to "take on the world." However, I found myself in a dilemma.

"Now, where do I go from here?" I asked myself. I wanted to do something but was, for some reason, unable to come up with anything that really excited me. The minute I thought of something that might excite me, my mind would negate it. I was in the state of boredom and was stubbornly resisting being there.

The more I tried to escape from my boredom, the worse it got. Once again I found myself in that squirrel cage of indecision, and it wasn't a very good feeling.

"I don't need this," I muttered. However I knew I needed help and asked. Immediately this channeling from Spirit began:

So, life is boring? You say that you are in a funk. Your thoughts have been scattered as you run helter-skelter trying to escape what you seem to feel is a fate worse than death.' Did you not know that Boredom is a very high and wonderful energy?

It is a friend, not an enemy. It can be the kick in the pants that will get your creative juices flowing. Why not allow it to do just that?

The culprit in this experience is not boredom, but your own stubborn resistance to being in that state of mind. Thus, instead of allowing this wonderful friend to enter your reality, you fight it tooth and nail—resisting it instead of inviting it into your domain.

This in turn sets up blockages in your creative abilities, and causes your thoughts to scatter like leaves blown by the wind. Thus you become unbalanced, which in turn leads to the feeling of being tired, depressed, confused, unable to cope—to get out of the trap you feel you are in.

Relax, breathe deeply, allow yourself to become the boredom with NO resistance. Once the resistance has been put to rest then the confusion—the wanting to dart here and there—will also vanish as will the boredom.

You then will find yourself relaxing, entering the sacred temple of your heart, where love for all resides, and where there is no judgment. Then all becomes equal and joy reigns supreme.

As I was receiving this message, I felt myself relaxing into the reality of what was being said, and found I was no longer resisting nor was I bored. Judgment sets up our stubborn resistance. It is our resistance, which stops us from creating. This then brings on boredom. Remove the judgment, and the rest will follow in its footsteps.

Evidently I had shot up from feeling the negative entrapment of the past trauma to the high vibration of boredom. This can happen when one finds that there are no more dragons to slay. It's like "ho hum, now what can I do?" That is when, if allowed, the creative juices can really flow.

By the way, this process can be used whenever anything negative comes up, be it depression, sadness, pain, or any judgment. All one has to do is to stop resisting and allow themselves with love to relax into the feeling. It works. I know, for I use it all the time, and as I have often said, *what you resist will persist* is very true.

My stubborn resistance has, at times, blocked my being able to advance as fast as I might have, had it not gotten in the way. It can create many forms of illness, such as blockages in the arteries, the intestinal track, or wherever blockages occur within the emotional and physical bodies, as well as the mental. This is an indication that one is not flowing freely within their own natural vibration of love.

The lesson, of course, is to listen with your heart and to allow your own knowingness to dictate what is right for you and what is not. Once you come from your heart, then there is no room for stubborn resistance. You do whatever you feel called to do—not what someone tells you they think you should do. For the heart always knows.

GOD DOES NOT JUDGE!

He/She
leaves that up to those who have
less understanding and compassion

SOUL MATES, LOVERS AND
WORTHY OPPONENTS

When there doesn't seem to be a beginning, where does one begin? What do I remember about my Soul Mate? Not much, at least not physically. However, his essence lingers on and on, calling to mine. It is like a sad, joyous song, leaving me with a longing that sometimes turns into an ache, deep within. Yet at the same time there also is that feeling of love and joy, which keeps me forever searching for him.

Was this undying love, this deep longing for that essence, the unknown force that kept driving me into the arms of men whose vibration could never compare with his?

I'm certain now that every man I felt could satisfy that longing, that thirst—which I thought could be quenched through physical contact—would never be able to. For once you start remembering, even if it is only a shadow of a memory, that glorious ecstasy of being with your soul mate, all else pales in comparison.

Where and when did we separate? What split us apart? Did it happen during the taking of the DNA strands so long ago, and was the separation of the god/goddess within a reflection of that time? Somewhere, deep within my mind, lies the answers, but how do I access them?

MeAmba, my higher Soul Self, who is always guiding and assisting me, asked, "Why not start with what you remember, and go from there?"

"Good idea," I thought. Then my mind clicked into what I believe to be my first memory this lifetime of my Soul Mate, Golden Eagle. I remembered driving somewhere close to the Arizona-California border. A beautiful golden eagle was soaring above my car, so I stopped and got out to watch it.

Golden eagles have, as far back as I can remember, always held a sort of fascination for me. Their gracefulness and beauty called to me to watch them whenever they appeared. In fact, I always felt a sort of kinship toward them and greeted them with a loving "Ho, brother!" This I had learned from time spent with Medicine Man Hawk and Morning Dove—to honor all creatures, great and small.

I stopped the car, got out, and was enjoying the show he was putting on. Suddenly this poem started coming to me, which slowly began opening the door to my memory of him—my Golden Eagle. It gave me a glimpse of another time, another place, when we were together.

He was a Golden Eagle, with dark piercing eyes
That held the wisdom of the ages.
He came to me one day, offering his friendship
And being my friend, he took no more than I could freely give
For in his wisdom, he knew the truth of giving
We spent happy days, bright with laughter
But before human emotion could forever enslave him
He spread his mighty wings and soared
High above the clouds
Standing on a towering crag, proud and alone,

He folded his wings, as in a benediction
And with Love and Compassion deep in his eyes
Looked down upon us, the poor earth-bound creatures
Left standing immobile, staring upward
In awe and envy

Of course, at that time, I wasn't aware that this would be the beginning of reuniting with my Soul Mate—the door to that long forgotten memory was just starting to open and only slightly. However, more was to follow.

It wasn't long after that I had this dream-like vision. I was in a beautiful deep green forest with other people, who looked like Indians, adorned in animal skins and bright colored feathers. It was nothing like any forest that I have encountered. However, it did have some resemblance to the rain forests of South America.

A tall, gorgeous man whose energy seemed to be vibrating at an extremely high level was there. He apparently was a great leader with fantastic knowledge, and I was his mate, working with him—healing and teaching. Together we were doing magical things for those around us. Then, for some reason that I couldn't understand, he was explaining to me why he had to leave, and that I must continue the work we had started. Then the vision cleared, and I found myself back in my bedroom, alone.

Was he my Soul Mate? Had he and I been separated in a far earlier time, and had I somehow gotten myself stuck within the Illusion, while he escaped? And, most important of all, has he visited me from time to time, and then had to leave in order not to also be trapped here on Earth again? Questions, questions, questions, for which I had very few, if any, answers.

I remember a time, shortly after Jimmy's death, when I was sitting in my living room in Paonia, reading *The Channelings of Bashar,* which was a favorite of both Jimmy's and mine. I was still feeling the deep grief from my son's death and was trying to make some sense of the whole scenario.

Suddenly a name started appearing across the page I was reading. It was very large, covering up the smaller print of the book. Staring in amazement at the word that appeared—SHA LANDA—I felt puzzled, yet somehow happy. This was a feeling that I hadn't experienced since my son's death. Who was ShaLanda? Was someone trying to get some kind of a message to me? Could it be Jimmy?

As I sat there, I began seeing the times that I had not been there for him during his childhood. How I so desperately tried to assist him after he had gotten really hooked on drugs. I remembered the many times of standing by him while others would deride me for doing so— those who didn't know the whole story of other lifetimes, as well as this one. They just didn't understand.

Somehow, I always felt that I would be able to find a way to pull him out of his addiction, and that once again he would be whole. I had seen the proof many times of how the Awakenings raised his vibration. This would last until his body would scream for drugs, sending him plunging back down into the abyss again. Now I know this was his path, his commitment before going on. He was experiencing, learning and teaching me in the process.

He was also touching the lives of others in his own way, reflecting and bringing forth what they needed to look at and release.

However, this night my faith in the Awakenings was shaken. Doubting them and myself, I silently asked, "Did I cause Jimmy to take his own life by giving him those Awakenings?" I sat there, trembling from the thought.

Then I heard Jimmy's familiar voice answering my unspoken question. "No, Little Mommy, not at all. In fact, the Awakenings were what freed me from that body in which I had gotten so stuck. And, believe me, I was really stuck.

The Awakenings raised my awarenes. I knew that unless I did something to extricate myself from that drug-ridden body, I soon would be trapped. Without my awareness, my knowingness, I would be nothing except a body, and both of us have come too far to let that happen. Thus I created a scenario that would let me escape."

Again I knew that I had been given the truth, and that death, in its own way, is also a healing. Much later I was given a channeling by Archangel Michael, which confirmed this. He said:

Life in any form is precious. The name of the game is to always take responsibility for whatever you choose to create within your life.

All death is a form of suicide. There are lessons to be learned on every level of existence, which is always done through experiencing in one form or another—i.e. through observation or putting yourself in the middle of any given scenario.

Some of these scenarios may be very difficult, depending on what viewpoint you are viewing them from—physical or spiritual. Each time you begin a new life, you have—before coming into the physical—committed yourself to experience certain scenarios for your growth, understanding, and to enhance your own power of love and light. For understanding and loving everything as being equal is the highest goal of all.

However, if the program you have committed yourself to becomes more than you can achieve—biting off more than you can chew—then you may find yourself believing you are a body, not a powerful, magnificent spirit living in a body. This is when you begin feeling trapped, lost, wanting to give up.

He then went on to say that you, the spirit, will make a choice and will either leave the body or decide to ride it out. He also said that there is no judgment except that which you place upon your own actions. **God does not judge. He/She leaves that up to those who have less understanding and compassion.**

There was, of course, more, which I won't go into at this time, so on with my story. Now more questions were rising within me. Who was ShaLanda, and what did Jimmy have to do with my Soul Mate, and when, if ever, would I really understand?

I have had many lovers, and have been with many Beings, both of the Light and the Dark, throughout my varied lifetimes. I have touched the lives of others and they mine, some of which have left indelible impressions.

The more I found out, the more I wanted to know. Such as, when we speak of soul mates are we speaking of an essence that weaves in and out of our many lifetimes, experiencing, assisting, and sharing? If so, is it because of the different "wrappings" they come in that we don't recognize who they really are, yet are attracted to their vibration?

I knew that I had been with that essence I knew as Jimmy many times before, and in many different scenarios. Some of which were, in my estimation, not very loving.

He was, at times, what one might call "a worthy opponent." But one thing of which you can rest assured is that I always learned. Then within those learnings would come an upswing in my awareness—perhaps not all at once, but I did learn. He was, as I have said before, a great teacher.

The last time I saw Jimmy, since his leaving the planet, was when I suddenly felt his energy calling me. Pausing for a moment to check into that energy, an opening between us occurred—a "parting of the veil."

There he was, in jeans and a shirt, leaning against what appeared to be a wooden fence. He was radiant. A gentle breeze was playing with his long, reddish-brown hair and beard. There seemed to be a golden glow all around him. He was smiling and looked so wonderful, so peaceful, as he gazed across a beautiful green landscape.

It was as if he were showing me that all was well with him, for which I am eternally thankful. All the past doubts, self-judgments, et cetera, have been erased. Now, whenever I think of him, it is that picture I see of Jimmy, my son, free at last.

One thing is for certain, that which I have experienced has enabled me to have a clearer picture of myself, and has assisted me greatly in living a far more optimum and ethical life than before. I guess you might say that the old saying "live and learn" was very apropos—at least for me.

Lovers I have had, lovers you have had—some good, some not so good. However, I bet that if we took the judgments off, we then would see just how much each has taught us and we them.

Of course, when we get the actual reason for having created the scenario, we then will understand the reason of why we did. However until we do, we will continue pulling in those who are more than willing to show up with their own negative bag of garbage. We then will either judge them or let go. However, if we do decide to let it affect us, it can act as a catalyst in clearing our own stuff.

Yes, they can be worthy opponents. However, we have attracted them to us, so thank them for their gifts instead of judging them. When we do, we stop dramatizing the scenario, and will let it go. Then they and their negative garbage will never darken our doorway again, unless we choose to bring them back.

Once the lesson is learned and understood, then there is no need to repeat it. Unless, of course, we get back into that same old "habitual-ritual." of judging. If so, the best advice is to drop it fast, and go on with something new, different, and more exciting—no use continuing riding a dead horse, it doesn't take one very far.

Still, there was no answer to my new batch of unanswered questions regarding ShaLanda, Jimmy, and my Soul Mate. Suddenly I got the hit to check out my god/goddess and child within.

I had been given a book, Dance of the Selves, which for some reason called to me. It made sense, since we are both male and female, that perhaps the reflections they were throwing at me had something to do with what I was feeling—separation, loneliness, anger, abandonment.

Upon doing this, I found that the god/goddess within—the male, female, a.k.a. as the yin and yang—were miles apart with mostly the female running the whole show, while the masculine part of me was withdrawn and silent. "So, what am I going to do about this?" I asked myself.

Remembering my Scientology training of being an Auditor—a listener with no judgment—and using my compassion and understanding, I went within, allowing each to have their say regarding how they felt. It was fascinating what came out. First, the goddess—or My Lady, whom he called her—had her say. He also called her a "pushy broad" later on, when it was his turn.

She was really into anger and blame at having to take over and perform both the creating and the manifesting, which she felt was "just like a man." Odd, but true, I always felt that I had to "carry the load," thus ending up supporting not only myself but the men I chose to bring into my life as well.

She also felt that he had abandoned her and had left her alone. She called him a wimp and a few other not-so-nice choice names. And she wanted someone more to her liking!

I could see that she was very headstrong, independent and judgmental. Wow, what a reflection of me—of what I had experienced and felt this lifetime, whenever I let a man into my life. I was beginning to see how the drama going on in my relationships with men was only a reflection of what I needed to look at within my own universe.

Perhaps I was being told to clean up my own act before reaching outside for someone to make me happy. Besides, no one can make someone else happy, for that is our own responsibility. They can, however, share happiness, which is the way it should be.

At first, these messages were very subtle, but became less subtle—more persistent—until I was forced to go within and recognize the source of my problems. Until we do, we continue bringing into our lives those who, through their part in the co-creation, reflect to us the true source of our troubles—be it the god/goddess within or whatever.

Waking up to the fact that there is trouble on the home front, i.e. god/goddess within, we then can unite them in peace and harmony. This action can lead to opening up the door for a wonderful relationship of sharing.

Needing someone to make us happy fades away and we find ourselves happily creating our lives without outside influence until that special someone appears to share our happiness.

Now it was Sir Charles turn, which she called him, or "Charlie" when she was in a coy, playful mood. He was much nicer, more polite, a little withdrawn. I sensed a sort of silent reserve about him, also fear and a feeling of confusion. Yet there also was a deep love for "My Lady."

He wanted reconciliation. She didn't. I then made it perfectly clear to both that they were going to have to work things out, for they were stuck for eternity with each other.

Then he started having his say. The separation evidently happened during the blocking off of the DNA strands. She felt he should have been her "knight in shining armor" and rescued her, stoping this from happening. He had a very hard time convincing her that he had been rendered as helpless as she, and that there was nothing he could have done.

Evidently she decided at that time to take over the whole operation of both manifesting and creating (the masculine manifests, while the feminine is the creating force).

So as time went by, she became more and more the dominating force, and he became less and less until his power was diminished to only a fraction of what it was. This could leave one feeling very lopsided, which I was until they came together in love and understanding.

What a revelation this was for me—the separating of the DNA which created the split between god/goddess, thus the two strands of DNA, pitted against each other, were being reflected in the many scenarios of my many lifetimes. Sometimes the dark side would dominate, and at other times the Light.

Anger and stubborn determination to survive, no matter what, seemed to be her main motivation. It was really becoming apparent to me of how I, as a female this lifetime, was playing out this scenario within. So now I was certain that there was a sort of common thread weaving from one lifetime to another.

I then got the feeling that perhaps the DNA scenario was when my Soul Mate and I also were separated so long ago. If so, perhaps this would also reunite me with my Soul Mate when my god/goddess came together in love and understanding.

So, the dialogue continued. It was a lot like a couple not talking to each other, but each would talk to me. Finally, after much talk with each blaming the other, oh yes, Sir Charles did lose his cool a few times, exploding all over "My Lady," the fireworks died down. That was when understanding of the situation that happened so long ago came into play.

First comes willingness to communicate. Then with communication comes understanding. Then, when that occurs love replaces judgment. Too bad our world leaders don't adhere to this universal truth. Then, instead of war and destruction, there would be peace and love, what a wonderful thought.

Now I have them communicating and working together as a team. The child, who is also a big part of each of us, or should be, took each of them by the hand and literally walked them into the love energy of the heart. Thus the family within has been united, and I feel peace and love where once there was turmoil and separation. Is that what Jesus meant when He said, *"And a little child shall lead them"*?

So again, I ask these questions: Is ShaLanda Golden Eagle really my true soul mate? I feel that he is. Was the essence that I knew as Jimmy this lifetime the same or a different essence?

Perhaps Jimmy was my twin, weaving in and out of many of my other lifetimes touching and teaching me? Whoever he was, he definitely was a "worthy opponent" on more than one occasion, as have I been his. I trust that I have assisted him, for I know he has me.

If he is my twin soul, choosing to experience the Dark of the Light this lifetime for my reflection, then that could explain our coming together lifetime after lifetime. There is a bond between twins that can never be broken, thus we are pulled together to assist each other on our path to enlightenment.

From what I remember of Bashar's teaching, there is a difference between a soul mate and a twin soul. The Twin Soul coming from the same Over Soul, or Higher Soul Self, while our Soul Mate is of a different Higher Soul Self. This would explain the sameness of vibration between Jimmy and me, and the overwhelming feeling when I think of ShaLanda. There definitely is a difference in my feelings toward Jimmy and ShaLanda. Who knows, I'm sure I don't. However, I can only relate that which is real to me.

I do know that whenever I feel ShaLanda Golden Eagle's energy, there is a feeling so strong that it becomes, at times, almost overwhelming. Has he come down into Earth's Illusion from time to time? Is he here in physical form now, and would I recognize him if he is?

All I know is that we, Jimmy and I, have been drawn together, lifetime after lifetime, assisting each other in various and unforgettable ways. I'm certain someday we will know all the answers, but for now I will have to rely on that which I know to be true for me, at this time.

I'm certain that the packaging ShaLanda would be in would be far different than what I remember him of being. After all, when we are not squeezed into a physical body on Planet Earth, we are far greater, bigger, more than what we appear to be, for then we are multidimensional.—reflecting our Whole Soul Selves.

So let us say for the sake of argument that our soul mates do appear from time to time in unfamiliar wrappings, playing different roles, and because of that we do not recognize them. Yet, their energy is so familiar that we are drawn to them, and they to us.

Perhaps we do come together, lifetime after lifetime, in order to assist each other up the path of evolvement. Just because that person is not packaged the way we think our soul mate should be, is it too preposterous to even imagine such a thing? I wonder!

MY MOONLIGHT LOVE

Come fly with me
Together, darling, we will touch the stars

"What is missing from my life?" I asked myself. I was busy enough doing Awakenings and channelings, but there was always that nagging little voice whispering "more, more, more."

"Less is better," I kept telling myself. I had done so much in raising my awareness, my vibration. Yet, no matter how many Awakenings I did, nor how many people I talked to, still that nagging little voice kept insistently saying, "Something's missing."

Once again I was feeling a tug at my heartstrings to see my Soul Mate—to feel him close to me. It had been so long since I had felt those strong arms sheltering me from the storms of life. Would I ever experience that feeling again?

I had tried other men's arms, and although the sex was great, still I was left with a sort of empty, lost, longing feeling. And so I knew that just any man would not take away the deep soul longing and loneliness, which became a sort of ache deep in my heart.

Will you ever come to me again, my darling? Oh, how I miss you. I could almost feel him close to me as I struggled to part the veil once again. But it was to no avail.

I could feel my vibration slowly lowering itself into the old pattern of Illusion's past. The longing, the sadness was becoming more predominant and I wasn't helping myself any by playing romantic music, daydreaming of those wonderful times of long ago.

I didn't particularly like experiencing emotions I no longer seemed to be able to control. Especially if they were bringing me back down into the Illusion once more. In other words, I was really getting into self-judgment, and it was starting to feel mighty uncomfortable. Once one is out of Illusion's low negativity, then returning to that area can become quite painful.

I needed something to raise my vibration and to get myself out of the soup. It really was bugging me. So, as the saying goes, "Ask and you shall receive," I asked. The answer came almost instantly via my good friend, Samuel.

Placing a brochure in my hand, he said, "Maybe this is what you need." I didn't even have to read it, for I knew, beyond a shadow of a doubt, that it was my next step in my evolvement. However, instead of being a step, it turned out to be a gigantic leap into higher awareness and vibration.

The brochure heading read DNA clearings. That was enough for me, for I had been told by MeAmba, my Higher Self, that this was an area that needed attention. I just wasn't certain how to go about doing it. I knew that there still was residue of negativity left on that one strand from long ago—mostly self judgment, which was deterring me from achieving what I wanted to Be, Do and Have in this lifetime.

So once again I called Selacia and made an appointment. The session was awesome, to say the least. Selacia spent an hour with me, working with The Council of Twelve. After the session, I began to notice tremendous awareness changes. My vibration was higher than ever, and no longer was I wallowing in what was. I was completely in the moment of each moment, and my body energy was ten-fold what it had been.

The Awakenings became very powerful, for I now was open to more of the Power of the Masters, Angels, and Guides. I could, almost instantly, see the hidden negative issues of those who came to me. Thus I was able to release them faster and easier than before. There also seemed to be more peace, more love, more of self understanding instilled within those receiving the Awakenings and in myself as well.

Of course, I thanked all who co-created this wonderful uplifting scenario with me, and knew I was on my way to new beginnings. 2001 was just around the corner.

Just before Christmas, my beautiful friend and constant companion, Thor, made his transition. I had the privilege of being by his side and opening the portal, so he could make his exit peacefully, which he did. We both knew it was time and so, with his exit, our commitment for this lifetime was over.

I was told by my guides to write the story of our life together, as he would be leaving sometime between Thanksgiving and Christmas. I completed the story and he left shortly after, on December 17. There is no sadness, only the joyous memories of a fourteen-year close relationship. Thor was, to say the least, the most wonderful dog I have ever known. Although I was never certain whether he was a dog or a master in a dog's body. I trust someday I will have the privilege of seeing him again—a cute little puppy, knocking at my heartstrings. I'd like that. This does happen with our animal guides. They do appear in physical form, and I know that this was not the first lifetime he has been with me.

It wasn't long after that I experienced something so beautiful, so fulfilling, that I would be hard-pressed to find the words that could express the intense emotions I felt.

It was deep in the night. I had been sound asleep and awoke to the beautiful strains of Debussy's Clair de Lune—the words were so beautiful, so full of love. I could hear myself saying them as the music played—*"You are my moonlight love, though you leave me, when stars fade away, come to me, my darling, make love to me in every way."*

Then I felt Him, my Soul Mate, ShaLanda. His beautiful essence was all around me. His hands gently caressing my body, as his lips claimed mine, traveling down my neck to my breasts, kissing my nipples, the valley that lay between.

Once again his lips claimed mine—long, beautiful, passionate kisses as my trembling body clung to his in the ecstasy of his embrace. His strong, lithe body gently massaging mine, lovingly.

I opened the door to my inner, most sacred chambers, and he entered, caressingly unlocking every part of me, touching and setting free my locked up emotions. Chills of excitement and ecstasy rippled through my body as we merged into each other, slowly moving to the dance of love.

Then the rhythm became a wild jungle beat as the warmth of our love burst into a flaming fire of passion and desire. As he thrust ever deeper, touching the very core of my being, the shackles of the Illusion fell away, together we soared higher and higher—two Golden Eagles, screaming our passion and our love, exploding into a million and one points of light, dancing among the stars.

Then, softly, gently, coming to rest in each other's arms, we were lost in the magical glow of our love, our passion, our ecstasy.

As the night gave way to the dawn, I felt his essence gently slipping away. My arms reached out to hold him close, to never let him go, and closed around emptiness.

Oh, how I wanted him to stay, to always be by my side. But he was of another dimension, where time does not exist. Then, as he vanished, I softly whispered, "Goodbye, my Beloved, until that wonderful moment when we never again will have to part.

"Until then, I will continue on my path and although I cannot see you, I know that you will always be with me, for we are one in our love—together forever."

if you don't like where you are going,
fire the chauffeur
and
put yourself in the driver's seat

LONELINESS, DRUGS, SEX, JUDGMENT,

EGO AND SUICIDE

Night draws her curtain around me
Leaving me lonely again
Making me wish I had someone to love
Or someone who'd just be my friend

I hear the soft sound of laughter
Like a whisper of love floating in
I close my eyes as I fight back the tears
God I could sure use a friend
Then loneliness comes walking in again

Oh those lonely people, where do they all come from? The Beetles
really had a way of expressing feelings in their music. I look around
and see so many whose eyes reflect their loneliness and fear—afraid to

join in. Wherever I go, they are always there reflecting to each other, yet unable to break through that barrier separating them.

My search to find the truth of who I am has taken me into some very interesting experiences. Some were dark and disturbing while others were exciting and wonderful. Each, in its own way, has assisted me greatly in rediscovering and claiming those many parts of me, which had fragmented and broken off along the path I had chosen to walk these many lifetimes.

Most of us have walked similar paths at one time or another, experiencing and judging, thus creating separation within ourselves. It is only when we bring back into our conscious memory those scenarios again, that we can release our judgments. We then are reunited with our fragmented parts, which I refer to as our children of the past, and in doing so we become whole.

How did I become so trapped within the Illusion? First, I would experience a scenario, either personally or by observing what others were experiencing, then I would judge it. The judgment was what stuck me in those scenarios, creating separation. Thus I left a part of me—my memory—behind, locking me into those scenarios. Had I loved the scenario for the experience, instead of judging, I would not have become fragmented in the first place.

However, sooner or later, comes the wake-up call to the fact that we have been there, done that, and also judged it. Then by removing the judgments, we find that there is no Karma to wade through for *Judgment creates our Karma. When there is no judgment, there is no karma.*

Why am I so certain of this? Because I have been there, done that and judged myself for doing it—fragmenting myself over my many lifetimes on Planet Earth. Since I can only relate my own experiences, I will do so. They may ring a bell of recognition, assisting you in recalling some of your own past so-called "transgressions" which you have judged.

Should painful or judgmental memories rise up, allow them to surface so they may be recognized and healed. However, if ignored and stuffed back down, the merry-go-round ride continues and sometimes in very disturbing and destructive ways.

What do I know of loneliness, drugs, sex, suicide, judgment and ego? Well, in recalling my many lifetimes here on earth, I have bumped up against each and they, in their own devious way, have pulverized me into oblivion more than once.

However, they have been what one might call worthy opponents and great teachers, as were the ones who co-created those scenarios with me. This lifetime seemed to be an accumulation of all of them returning, rising up to be remembered, and claimed as the children of my creation in order to be recognized and loved instead of judged. Thus, I have learned that to judge is not really the way to go. In fact, it can be quite detrimental.

Loneliness has been a constant companion of mine for a very long time. That horse's kick did create a separation within me, separating me from my knowingness and love. Confusion was also always around, causing me to walk the path of not knowing who I really was or why I was here. There was so much separation within me, no wonder I felt lonely and confused.

Back then I only knew I was lonely, but with no understanding of why. This sent me into experiencing scenarios that I somehow thought would fill that empty void—they never did.

I was asked by a special pen pal what made me lonely, sad, angry, or whatever affected me in a negative way? This started me looking into the reason of why I had experienced such negative emotions.

I must have been getting some kind of morbid enjoyment out of suffering. I remember playing sad music, and watching even sadder movies as I either drank myself into oblivion or cried myself to sleep. The crazy thing was that I didn't have a clue as to why I felt so lonely—so sad.

I never shared these feelings with anyone. When out with friends, rest assured that I always had my "happy face" on, covering up my real feelings, exchanging them for drinking and meaningless sexual experiences. However, after the fun and games, there still remained that haunting and lonely, empty feeling that would rise up and smack me right in my heart again.

Sex is wonderful and will, if entered into without judgment, alleviate the pressures of life to a great degree. However, it will not erase the emotional turmoil permanently, at least it didn't for me.

When our emotions are put aside and ignored instead of being understood and healed, then the need for more sex, more alcohol, drugs, or whatever we use to sidestep the real issue, will be there. It then will take over and become the driving force in one's life. It's not what we do, but our reason for doing it that creates the problem.

This can lead to some very harmful scenarios, for instead of coming from love and understanding there will be anger and emotional pain, driving one on and on in search of finding a balance, thus creating addiction.

When one is not at ease with ones self, then their negative emotions can be transmitted to their sexual partners, creating dis-ease in them as well.

This is a two-terminal universe and we do need others to love, communicate and share with. However, until we go within and clean up our own act, not many relationships will be able to endure that test and eventually will break up. This is when the loneliness engulfs us, then we are off and running again.

I kept playing that same old record over and over in different scenarios until finally waking up to what I was co-creating, and the reason behind it.

No one can heal our emotional body, the Inner Child, but ourselves. It is our responsibility, and to allow someone else to try to do it for us would not be fair to them or to ourselves. It would only result in failure and blame.

The longing to share is very ingrained in all of us. However, I have found that just anyone will not fill the bill. I can have others around who are, more or less, only bodies. However, unless there is that connection of compassion and understanding, then that wonderful feeling of oneness will be missing.

I've been alone all this lifetime. Yes, I have had companions, mates, and partners who shared some of me and I some of them. Yet there was always that separation, never the oneness.

I thought I was beyond those feelings of loneliness, but I was wrong—dead wrong. "I've gone so far, done so much and was vibrating at a very high level of awareness. How could I possibly have those kinds of feelings?" I asked myself. I was in denial and was soon to have my eyes opened—wide.

Suddenly I started becoming aware of wishing that I had someone special to share a cup of coffee, exchange ideas—to just be there. Driving home from an afternoon spent upon my beautiful Grand Mesa, I was listening to some romantic classical music and came upon a panoramic view of the valley below.

The sun was just starting to set, turning the sky into blazing colors of pink, lavender and gold. The scene was awesome. I turned into a scenic view pullout, stopped the car, drinking in the beauty of that spectacular scene as the music played, filling my senses to overflowing.

This was when I became aware of wanting someone to be with, just to hold my hand, touch me, share with me those sensuous feelings I was having—to feel, understand, become one, lost within that magical moment. Only the lonely will be able to understand that kind of longing, for if you haven't been there, how can you really understand?

Feeling this lost, lonely feeling coming over me, I started my car and headed home to a cold and empty house. My big dog, Thor, who had been my companion for almost fourteen years, had made his transition some two months before. Knowing that he wouldn't be there to greet me with a wag of his tail, looking at me with his big brown eyes as if to say "gee, I'm glad your home—what's for supper" only added to my misery.

I wanted to cry, but couldn't. I wanted someone to hold me and realized I had no one. "Oh God," I cried out, "why am I so alone. Why have I created this?"

I sank down into my reclining chair, feeling lost, abandoned—like a lonely little child. Then, I began to feel a warm, loving essence around me. It was as though strong, loving arms were cradling, nurturing me. I became lost in that loving energy—so warm, so comforting.

After some time, I became aware that the aching, lonely abandoned feeling was gone, as was that loving essence. However, for some reason, I felt fulfilled in every way. Once again, I was happy, content in knowing that I am never alone—none of us are. The oneness is always there. All we have to do is to open ourselves up to receiving it.

The fear of being alone and lonely plunges some into deep despair. Others try desperately to avoid those feelings by chasing aimlessly here and there, always searching for that elusive butterfly of their dreams in hopes of alleviating those feelings.

Loneliness can do weird things to people—hooking them on drugs, alcohol, promiscuous sex, and creating less than desirable relationships. Thus they cover up the real self with false personalities, creating more separation within.

I always thought that if I kept trying something new, it would eventually fill that empty void. It never did. For whenever the new became old, and it always does unless we stay in the moment, then I would find myself chasing after that elusive butterfly again.

The saying that nothing is new under the sun certainly is true. However, it all depends on how one looks at everything. Changing one's point of view can make everything new and exciting in any given moment. It's the old "habitual ritual" thinking that keeps the new and exciting outlook on life from happening.

Have I taken drugs? Of course, we all have, be it prescription or illegal. A drug is a drug, affecting our mental and physical bodies in various ways.

Why do we take them? I can't speak for you, but mine was to escape, from pain of the body, of the mind and of life. A drug's main and, in my opinion, only purpose is to escape or help us avoid that which we cannot face.

While in Scientology, I did what they called The Drug Rundown. This entailed hours of sweating in a sauna, heavy doses of vitamins, and auditing to take one back to past and present usage of all drugs. When you have cleared your emotional, mental and physical bodies of those memories, then they no longer have much impact.

Once completed, the feeling is quite extraordinary. The best way I can describe it is that my body felt like a clear mountain stream, free of pollution and contamination. That feeling didn't last but did stay for some time, acting as a guideline of how it should feel all the time.

I also realized that, as time went by, there was a change in my outlook as far as alcohol and drugs were concerned. No longer was I grabbing for them in order to escape from my "demons." This didn't happen all at once, but gradually as I continued on my path toward awareness.

While doing the auditing part, I touched in on many lifetimes of drug use and abuse. One in particular that stands out in my memory was that of being an old Oriental man, smoking my opium pipe. There was a sort of hopeless, nothing-mattered, going no place feeling while viewing that one. This, of course, is always the end result of trying to escape through drug use, be it alcohol or whatever one chooses to use.

Sex and certain drugs will give one that high feeling. However, since what goes up must come down, sooner or later one will either have to face their own demons or go soaring off again into the wild blue yonder by taking more drugs. This then sets up a craving for more and more in order to gain their so called utopia. It's not the drug, the alcohol nor the sex, but the reason of why we resort to using it excessively.

Some people can get hooked more easily than others—mostly because they are not able to or haven't faced themselves and their judgments. They then try taking the so-called easy way out.

While involved with my son's drug addiction, I wrote a song called COME AND DANCE. I'll never forget his reaction when I sang it to him. Tears came to his eyes and he said, "Boy, Mom, this really does describe the drug scene."

These are the lyrics:

She rode in on a flash of lightning as the thunder ripped open the sky
and I stared in silent wonder, for I was only a passer by
she was riding a stallion she called cocaine and a needle was sticking
deep in her vein
then she smiled as she sang her siren's song and like a fool, I danced along.

Soon others were dancing along with me as she increased her weird
wild beat
my body was numb and tired, but the rhythm still stayed in my feet
so she fed me again with the needle that she carried so deep in her vein
and once again I was laughing. it was crazy and I felt insane.

Then the dawn was breaking and everyone had gone
leaving me cold and shaking, still listening for her song
so whenever I hear her music, calling incessantly
I follow her as if in a trance, my body is tired but yet I must dance on
*   through eternity.*

Listen to the music of the siren, listen to the song she sings so well
promising the things you've always dreamed of
now you've a one-way ticket straight to hell
Come and dance. Come and dance.
*   COME AND DANCE!*

I know that we all create, with the assistance of others, everything that we experience. As for me, I can't say that I am sorry for what I've created—no regrets. However, I am very confident that there are easier ways of finding one's true vibration than the path I chose to explore. It just happened to be the path I chose to walk.

Past life experiences also play a part in this. The bottom line is how much judgment have we heaped upon ourselves and how willing are we to face them and bring them forward for understanding and release.

Until doing this, I actually felt undeserving of anything and didn't know why. I now know that which I judged as being dark, devious and unforgivable was only that which I had chosen to experience with the assistance of others. However, life would have been so much easier for me had I known.

Drugs, unless we are very aware, will lead us down paths that promise peace, awareness, and power—all of those wonderful things we feel we don't possess. However, after dancing to their music, we find we are back in the rat race once again, more unsure of ourselves than before.

Never underestimate the power of the lower dark vibrations. Its game is to divide and conquer through fear, doubts of self and of God, leaving us with feelings of insecurity, pain—both mental and physical—taking us on that roller-coaster ride.

When this occurs, we usually grab for anything or anybody that we believe will balance us. At that point in my life, I wasn't very selective in who or what I grabbed.

Of course, had I not judged myself or bought other's judgments, then I would have regained my balance. Instead, I decided to explore the dark shadowy side of myself with more drugs—alcohol was my choice—and promiscuous sex, which, of course, threw me even more off balance.

Sooner or later, we do get the message. This usually comes after we have experienced all we care to on that shadowy side of self. Rising above Illusion's negative reflection, I started seeing that I did have choices as to what I wished to experience. Upon making the decision to let go of all my judgments and loving myself unconditionally, I now partake and enjoy the wonderful banquet of life without guilt or blame. However I do use discernment as to what is for my highest good. This everyone will do when they are ready.

Self-esteem plays a big role in what we choose to experience. I once asked a girl why she turned to drugs. Her answer was "I wasn't anybody and I wanted to be somebody so I became a druggie."

This was quite a reflection for me—it really rang a bell. Of course, Unconditional Love is always the bottom line. So, when I began to understand myself, I then let go of my judgments, replacing them with love and compassion for all I had put myself through. I did this without feeling sorry for myself—not even a little bit.

As a friend once told me, the words sorry and sympathy lie somewhere between shit and syphilis in the dictionary. These words carry a very low vibration, so instead of sympathizing or feeling sorry for someone, or myself, I use empathy, understanding, and compassion. This keeps me above those low vibrations, lifting those who feel that they are victims higher as well.

Many of us become trapped in those low vibrations for, according to society, sympathy is the proper way to respond to those playing victim, and so we continue to perpetuate that which would be better for all concerned if thrown into the "no longer does this serve me" pile. However, do use compassion and understanding.

I refuse to adhere to the past conceptions of anything that is no longer for my highest good. Otherwise I am only digging the hole deeper, making it harder for me to crawl out of.

One incident of experiencing drugs and observing the end result of judgment and suicide happened while living in the Los Angeles area.

A group of friends got together to experience the drug E or Ecstasy—so called because of its reputation of taking those who tried it to higher levels of awareness, or so they thought.

I was invited to join the group so, like the song said, danced along. I tried it twice. The first time I could hardly move. My back went out on me and I was so helpless, my son, who had also joined in the dance, had to literally carry me to the car. As for that wonderful, high feeling, I never achieved it—only pain and a hangover.

However, being a "die-hard," I decided to try it again. This time I was more alert and noticed the leader of the group would come in and take a woman off to a private room. After some high yells of releasing and sobbing, back she would come and another would go in. One came back with her pants half down.

It was my turn, so in I went, not knowing what to expect. It seemed as though I was not in my body, but watching the scenario from a distance. He had me sitting with my legs spread apart. However, that was as far as it went. Either he had run out of bullets or my Guardian Angel would let me have no part of that scene. It could have been both.

That night, after I got home and was in bed, someone came to me—it might have been Bashar or MeAmba—and asked me if that was really what I wanted to experience, to give my power away again. My answer was a definite NO! I had come too far for that to happen, so I never went back.

I knew beyond a shadow of a doubt that drugs of any kind were not for me. Besides, I had flown higher, felt more complete, more love in my meditations with the Angels and Masters than any drug could or had ever taken me. Besides, there was never any downslide afterwards. I never went back, but returned to the safety and sanity of Bashar's wonderful counseling. However, they continued that scenario for some time. The leader of this group may or may not have been guided by the channel for Leah—he was her right-hand man.

However it all ended abruptly one Saturday morning when he went to a secluded area, took a gun and blew his brains out. Somehow his ethics got all screwed up with drugs, thus creating the sex scenario. Had he looked upon it with no judgment, he might still be alive today, enjoying his wife and baby that he left behind.

However, there are no mistakes as we each choose our path to walk. So it was as my son has said over and over again, "Take the judgment off, for everything is perfect just the way it is in each moment for our evolvement."

Those who participated in that scenario learned, and evolved in their own way. The big culprit, in my estimation, is judging whatever we have chosen to experience instead of loving the experience and moving on.

I have been told over and over, *Experience, yes—judge, no!*

It does pay to be aware and discerning what is for our highest good. I was also told, *If you don't like where you are going, fire the chauffeur and get in the driver's seat,* which has been very good advice for me.

This makes me aware that I am responsible for choosing whatever I am experiencing. I now choose with discernment the way I want my life to unfold.

One thing I cannot be is unethical in my dealings with others, for when I am, then I am also being unethical to myself. We all know when we are not living up to the Universal Code of Ethics. We may try to kid ourselves into thinking we don't. However, when we go against that which we know to be true, it can get us into a lot of unnecessary trouble. But, if you need the lesson, then go for it.

What would have happened to me had I continued on the path of alcohol and drugs? This I don't know, and am thankful I didn't have to find out, for I am very happy with me the way I am today.

Sex is good. In fact, it's great when used in the right way—i.e. whatever turns you on without judgment. We have been given many wonderful gifts to use, either to enhance or to destroy ourselves. As Bashar has said so many times—*Our Choice, Always.*

Sex can also be a controller. Many a person has become so obsessed with it that they let it be their "all," believing it is the answer to whatever they wish to escape from. This never works for it can consume one's life, and the actual problem never gets handled.

It is a great release but, like anything else used to excess, will eventually deter us from our path of knowing all of our many-faceted self. Thus, we end up exploring only one part, leaving the rest of us strewn along the path of forgetting who we really are.

Eventually, the thrill gets less and less. Then what was once a beautiful and spiritual expression turns to lust—mostly because it wasn't honored and integrated with our spiritual and emotional self. Thus, we become unbalanced. The Universe is always within its balance. It has to be or it would destroy itself. Since we are a part of the universe, we also have to be within our own balance. Otherwise, we end up destroying ourselves—our lives in various ways.

Since my DNA strands of awareness have been restored, I have been exploring the separation created by Illusion's false god, which also created separation within myself. This created judgment, guilt, and fear of self-expression, limiting my ability to be who I truly am.

Sex is a great example of this for it sets up a resistance to, and a longing for at the same time. Religions have played a great part in this dilemma with their interpretations of what their god is telling them is sinful. Thus they control with judgment, instead of using love and awareness. In doing this, the sex act has been hidden, put to shame, creating all kinds of emotional and also mental problems.

The truth is that the Great I AM—the true and only God—has placed a banquet before us to enjoy without self-guilt, resistance or judgment.

However, if we become gluttonous and over-indulge by using anything as a way to escape from ourselves, it will create an imbalance within our own universe and we will suffer until we regain our balance. This is not a punishment by God for over-indulging. It is just a warning from our all-knowing Higher Self to return to balance. *The True God Does Not Punish Nor Judge.*

Perhaps if we released all of our judgments, control and loved unconditionally all things, especially ourselves, then we permanently would be balanced within our own universe, thus assisting the planet to also stabilize.

THROUGH THIS MYTH WE CALL ILLUSION

Real love is almost unheard of here, for true love has no judgments
and no conditions. *IT IS BECAUSE IT IS* and needs no qualifications
for being.

While exploring this "forbidden fruit" phenomenon, I was given
this message by Spirit of Enlightenment, which helped to open my eyes
to some of the reasons of why the children on Planet Earth are so
screwed up. It started out by saying:

I am with you. You are never alone. Love everything, unconditionally.

*It is the judgment that created the connotation that something is good
or bad. This may stem from past programming and scenarios, creating core
incidents. It may also be genetic beliefs passed down from other generations
regarding religion and racial prejudice. Rise above all of this and see
everything as equal.*

*Your world would be a much more peaceful, happier place if the sexual
experience was accepted in its entirety, without judgment. The only sexual
act that should never be created is when one is forced to participate against
their will.*

*However, even those kinds of acts would eventually disappear off of
the planet if sexual pleasures were not suppressed. It is the judgment and
suppression that creates the negative. WHAT ONE RESISTS WILL
PERSIST.*

*Your so-called "whore houses," which the more highly aware refer to as
"release houses," should be accepted into your society, for they do play an
important role in assisting in releasing inner turmoil on your planet today.
It is the judgments placed upon such places by the majority, including your
governments and religions, that is creating stress and dis-ease in place of
peace and tranquillity.*

*If accepted in the light of love, the sexual act, in whatever form it is
created, would then be lifted out of judgment and placed within the realms
of high esteem. It then would be accepted with no judgment. This would
free Earth's children to explore in whatever way they wished without fear
of condemnation or ridicule.*

*When this does occur, then anger, revenge and harmful acts of crime,
including molestation and rape, would soon disappear, for when judgment
is no more then love becomes the predominant factor.*

In other words, when all of humanity's negativity is released, eventually love would become deeper, wider, more meaningful. The true meaning of love is rarely experienced on Planet Earth at this time.

The physical body is beautiful and needs the release through sexual pleasures as much as it needs food. Thus, there should be no controls, no guilt—only the wonderful freedom of expression for a shared moment of the ecstasy of fulfillment.

The resistance to the sexual experience has been a part of the control established by the false god and perpetuated by its followers. The time is at hand for all truth to be revealed not just part of it.

Woman and men are equal and should be allowed to revel and share their equality without judgment or shame.

Furthermore, if the two individuals are of like vibration in their love and light—spiritually, mentally, emotionally and physically—then the experience can and will be beyond description.

It is up to each individual to take responsibility in deciding what they wish to experience. Otherwise, self-judgment and blame may enter the picture. Also one must honor the other individual's choice with love, understanding and compassion and with no judgment.

I then asked, "Is there a difference in the mental, physical, emotional and spiritual make-up of the hetero and homo-sexual?"

The sum and total answer lies in choices and what one has committed to experience each lifetime. It is another way of the Soul experiencing itself. There is, due to the teachings of the "judgmental false god" on Planet Earth, much stigma and condemnation placed on those who choose to come and reflect to others the Truth of The Great I AM—ALL IS PERFECT IN WHATEVER WAY ONE WISHES TO EXPRESS ONE'S SELF.

Many of Earth's children are so stuck in judgment and condemnation that they refuse to budge from their fixed ideas and will defend to the death those beliefs.

To each his own should be everyone's motto, thus allowing freedom of expression for everyone without shame or blame and without trying to force others to conform to their beliefs.

Many have been programmed to see everything one way, judging those who are "different." This will create resistance against any minority group, inflicting pain—both mental and physical—in order to prove that they are right and the others are wrong. They are reflecting the powerful control and judgment of "the false god."

They have been so heavily programmed that they do not realize that in THE GREAT I AM's eyes there is no right or wrong. Thus everything and everyone is precious and loved unconditionally for the experiences they have chosen to walk through.

Also, when one is praying to the Great I AM, asking that they be extricated from whatever scenario they have created, you can rest assured that will not happen. The Great I AM, in Its Eternal Wisdom, knows that if you have the power to create a certain scenario, you also have the power to uncreate it. Why would God interfere with your Free Will?

There will always be Masters, Angels, and Guides around to assist and strengthen you with loving energy from that awesome and powerful Source. It is there for everyone. However, you must be willing to let go of any ego and stubborn resistance, surrendering and allowing yourself to receive that gift. Most of you are so caught up in resistance that you block yourself from receiving that which you ask for. Trust and letting go is what will make it so.

So to answer your question, it is not the act itself but the way one perceives and judges it, for all is perfect in GOD'S eyes.

"How can one know when one is about to engage in a scenario that might not be for one's highest good and evolvement?" I asked.

Since everything is experience, there is no right or wrong. However, this can become very tricky unless one is in total balance within. When within one's balance, then the awareness of the true meaning of right and wrong will come to light. This will assist you greatly in understanding those two vibrations.

The key to all things is vibration—i.e. the matching of vibrations is crucial to how you feel regarding others in respect to self. Do you feel joyful, peaceful or agitated and nervous? The closer you are in vibration to those around you, the more likely you will feel the joy and the peace. In other words, some vibrations will feel highly compatible while others will grate against your own in an uncomfortable way.

When a certain person or scenario is not for your highest good, you then will feel a vibration from your Higher Self. Some call it a gut feeling or intuition. It is a signal to be discerning. The finer tuned you are to your source, the sooner you will become aware of that signal.

185

Your awareness comes from recognizing and releasing your negative fears, doubts and judgments. These lower vibrations can and will cloud your connection to your Higher Soul Self. The more you release those low vibrations, the more you become love and light. This raises your vibration and awareness connecting you to your source—out of Illusion's grasp.

When this occurs, you will know almost instantly what is, and what is not for your highest good. This is called discernment. One must learn to stop, listen and check out the vibrations before entering any scenario. You then will know when to say yes and when to say no. Wishing you joyful experiencing, I AM SPIRIT OF ENLIGHTENMENT.

I am in full agreement with all that Spirit revealed to me. There have been so many crimes committed through sex acts of less than a loving vibration. Hidden sex thoughts, manifesting into anger, rape, child molestation, torture—the list goes on and on.

No one should molest or hurt anyone, especially a child. They need loving guidance, support and understanding so they will grow into responsible adults. They then will have the ability to make their own decisions out of unconditional love for themselves and others. They are reflections of ourselves, and should be treated the way we would like to be treated.

The Indigo Children have now arrived, and have cleared the way for the Crystal Babies to come aboard. Both, in their own way, are bringing much light and knowledge to the Planet. They are teaching and reflecting to us that when we let go of our judgment, loving unconditionally all things—especially ourselves—then, and only then, will there be true peace for us and our beautiful planet. So support and listen to these wonderful little powerful Beings of Light. They have much to teach us, for as was foretold so long ago *"A little child shall lead us."*

you may think that you do not know the
answers on this physical level,

However,
as a Master you always know so
Honor the Master that you are
And refuse to play the Victim Game

PLAYING THE MASTER/VICTIM GAME

Is it possible to be both, simultaneously? In one sense, I am certain I have been. It all depends on how we view ourselves, and from whose viewpoint. As a child and most of my adult years, I have always felt limited. Yet, for some unexplainable reason, I also felt that I was more than what I was able to touch in on. It was as though I were only a silhouette of who I felt I really was. Thus, most of my life has been spent in confusion.

Bashar explains confusion as one who is trying to co-fuse their many separated parts. When that is accomplished, then confusion is no more. This has been very true for me—I no longer walk in confusion about anything. I may not know on this level, but I always know that I know on some level, and sooner or later the total picture will appear. The trick is to know that you know. Then relax and allow the picture to complete itself. In doing so, I no longer buy the considerations of others.

Confusion has always played a big part in the way I lived my life until now. However, it has allowed me to explore life in different ways, and has also broadened my horizons considerably. Thus my awareness and compassion has also taken on a more expanded view of others as well as myself.

My knowingness tells me that, if I had not been kicked in the head by that horse so long ago, I probably would not have gone looking for my many missing fragments. However, I did go searching, and my search did pay off. I now recognize and love the Master that I am, instead of pretending I am a victim.

I've been knocked down more times than a king pin in a bowling alley, only to find myself again standing up, ready to take on the world, and whatever it chose to throw at me. Then, about the time I began having some self confidence in myself, *WHAM!* here would come that darn ball again.

Evidently, I had somehow placed myself on the wrong side—if there is such a thing as wrong—thus allowing myself to be knocked down. However, upon taking a more extended point of view, perhaps I was experiencing both sides at the same time—being the cause as well as the effect. When I look at it that way, am I really a victim, or a master playing at being a victim?

That part, which left when I was a small child, seemed to be the all-knowing and all-loving part of me—the master that I somehow knew I was, yet was unable to be. Thus from one viewpoint it appeared as though I were a victim. All I know is that back then I felt unsure, unworthy and unloved without a clue as to why. This allowed me to experience how it feels to be a victim. However, by doing this, I also shut down my own knowingness of what I was creating as a Master.

Since experience is always the name of this game we call life, then isn't it how I, you, or anyone chooses to play the game that counts, allowing ourselves to do so with no judgment or criticism?

Perhaps you are thinking, "This is ridiculous, for no one can be both," but is it? When we think in terms of limitation, then are we not playing the game of being limited instead of limitless

This concept of being both master and victim at the same time would definitely make me the captain of my own ship—my own destiny. It would also make more sense of why we were given Free Will, thus making us think twice before entering into scenarios that were not for our highest good. Since Free Will is God's gift to us, or so we have been told, then when we decide to act out both sides of the polarities of being both master and victim isn't that using that wonderful gift in a broader spectrum?

From my viewpoint, I have never been a victim. I have just been allowing myself to explore all of who I am and will be. Thus, upon viewing myself in this way, I can position myself into creating a more optimum, enjoyable life. This I am now doing, and I intend to continue doing by using discernment and taking responsibility for what I choose to create—thus I no longer give my power away

Everything we do to or for ourselves, or others, has a direct effect upon our own lives, placing us in either a lower or higher vibration. Thus it does pay to walk within the Universal guidelines of integrity and ethics at all times. This is the mark of a true Master, and taking on the role of a master will open the doorway to endless possibilities.

Have I received my Mastership yet? No, but I'm working on it. One thing I know for certain is that if I allow myself to get into judgment, then I have not come as far as I would like to think I have. And this means judgment about anything. I can observe to my heart's content what is happening in my reality as well as in others. However, if I become judgmental regarding the scenario, whatever it may be, I then become involved, whether I want to or not.

There have been many instances on Planet Earth of Masters playing the victim game for reflection and teaching. Each chose some kind of a traumatic scenario in order to get our attention, and to teach us to observe the pitfalls of becoming a victim. This is what Masters do when they come onto our Planet—create a traumatic scenario, trusting that it will open us up to remembering our own commitment. We then would be able to see the Masters we truly are, creating our own victimhood.

However, instead of rising to the occasion by loving the scenario, unconditionally, we judge it, and get caught up in Illusion's dramatization with our judgments. When we don't get the lesson, we then re-create similar scenarios until we do.

We do this by trying to take on others' responsibilities, and sticking our noses into other people's scenarios. Then, when we fail, we make ourselves victims with our misguided thoughts of guilt, blame, and self-condemnation for not being able to "save" those whom we felt were being victimized.

The Masters were always able to rise above the Illusion. They knew that they, and they alone, were creating those scenarios, and also the reason for creating them. Thus there was no judgment on their part. However, we failed to recognize that they were Masters creating their own victimhood. We only saw them as victims, and the lesson was lost in judgment.

So we continue taking on the responsibilities of others in order to rid ourselves of our own self-imposed feelings of guilt, shame, and self-condemnation. Thus we continue perpetuating the game of victimhood by seeing others as victims with our judgments. These reflections then make us victims, as well. We do this by dramatizing and maximizing the negative, while minimizing the positive—the negative being victimhood, the positive being Masters. Once we see everyone as Masters, creating whatever for experience and evolvement, then this game will cease to exist.

A great example of the Master/Victim game is the one set up by Lord Jesus while on Planet Earth. He was and still is a great Master, who created a game of such magnitude that it has been indelibly written, and carried in our memories since that long ago era.

However, did we really get His beautiful message of Unconditional Love? Evidently not, for how many of us still are walking in our judgments of ourselves and others? I am certain that we all know, or should know, *that you cannot judge and love at the same time—it is impossible.* His message was to LOVE, not judge

When He was on the cross and said *"Father, forgive them. For they know not what they do."* He was not asking for forgiveness for what they were doing to him through that co-creation. He was a Master, and knew that He was responsible for calling in those to co-create with Him that scenario.

Who then was He asking forgiveness for? It was for all of those who judged, and are still judging to this day regarding that scenario. We continue blaming Judas, and the Roman authorities for their participation in that which The Master, Lord Jesus, came here to create. After all, it was His Free Will and his Intention to create that traumatic scenario for its affect upon Planet Earth. However we have been unable to rise above Illusion's entrapment—we are too weighted down with our self-condemnation, guilt feelings, blame and shame. He came here to teach us Unconditional Love, and we have failed the lesson miserably with our judgments.

Religions have had a lot to do with perpetuating the judgment. I remember as a small child, sitting in the front row pew of a church, as a preacher pounded on the pulpit. Then pointing an accusing finger at us—I was certain it was directly at me—in a powerful unloving voice said, "HE DIED FOR YOUR SINS. YOU PUT HIM ON THAT CROSS!" I cowed in my seat at the thought. It sounded to me, in my confused state, that he was almost screaming those words. It was very forceful and did re-enforce my own guilt feelings of this and many lifetimes.

How many of us have been brain-washed, in one way or another, until we felt that we were "Guilty as charged?" But are we really guilty, or was all of this used to manipulate us into forgetting that we also are Masters? Of course, He was only playing out His role as creator of that scenario, as were all the others who were involved.

Yes, we have been controlled and manipulated by our own, as well as others' misplaced judgments, all of which has assisted us greatly in exploring the negative side of ourselves.

However, the time has come for clarification of our role in taking on others' responsibilities. We need only be responsible unto ourselves, and walk in our own integrity, with no judgment. Otherwise we will never be free to become the Masters that we are. *Masters Love Unconditionally—Victims and controllers judge.*

Yes Lord Jesus was and is a powerful Master, able to appear and disappear at will. This He could have done at anytime by extracting Himself from that scenario. In fact, he did, or at least that is what I was told by Mother Mary. The following is what she revealed to assist me in understanding the true purpose and message behind The Crucifixion.

"Father, forgive them for they know not what they do!" How true these words for had they all been aware of the Illusion, and its dramatization,

then they would have loved the scenario and themselves, unconditionally. Thus there would have been no need for the deed.

However, Jesus knew the role He was to play in order to break through the illusion of death, pain, and suffering. So allowed Himself to be the major player in that scenario. This was his main purpose in coming into Planet Earth's Illusion which had entrapped so many of Her children in its negative snare.

So, as a very high Master, He volunteered His Services in order to break through the false conception of death and judgment. Did He actually suffer and die? Of course He did not. For a Being of that magnitude can, through raising His/Her vibration, leave the physical body and rise out of harms way of pain and suffering.

The physical body, of course, did feel the trauma, and dramatized the scenario, as written in The Divine Plan. Thus, when it felt the departure of that powerful Spirit leaving, the physical body cried out "My God, My God, why has Thou forsaken me?" Which then created doubts, bringing up the judgment of those who were seeing only that which was apparent, not the complete picture.

Had those who witnessed this scenario over 2,000 years ago looked upon it through the eyes of love instead of judgment, many would have walked out of their self-imposed imprisonment on Planet Earth, becoming Masters of Light. However, since that didn't happen back then, the Light of Truth must now be revealed in order for Earth's children to rise above their judgments and fears of pain and death, and take their chosen place above the Illusion.

Once all of you have released your judgments, loving yourselves and each other, unconditionally, then will the light of Earth shine like the brightest star in the Heavens, as Mother Earth becomes the brilliant Light she is destined to be.

So clean up the garbage within you, for what you see happening on the outside is only a reflection of what you each are creating with your judgments and fears.

Go My Children, judge not, but love unconditionally and the New World for which you have been hoping, praying, and dreaming about will be a reality. There is work to be done, but it must be done within each of you—not outside of yourselves. The only tool you need to clean up this beautiful planet is your Unconditional Love for all and everything, but most of all for yourself. This is the true message of Lord Jesus and all of the other Masters of Light, who are always with you, as am I.

I AM MOTHER MARY OF THE MOTHER GOD ESSENCE.

This makes more sense to me. Jesus was a Master in control at all times of the scenario He was creating. Thus He reflected to all of us the games that go on within the Illusion with its dramatization, containing lies and half-truths. This is how, through our judgments, we have clouded our memories of being the Master, as we play the Illusion's game of victimhood.

Had we only been more observant, perhaps our path would not have been so traumatic and painful. Observation means just that, looking at a scenario without becoming emotionally involved or having it bring up our "stuff." Being critical of how someone else is walking their path is judgment and nothing less. When we judge we then will become emotionally involved in the scenario, and it just may not be what we should be experiencing at this time for our highest good. Besides, our emotions, unless cleared of judgment, can give us a "blind side," distorting the actual truth.

I know that my physical body does need more clearing, and I am still in the process of understanding it completely. I am becoming more in communication with it, and have made giant leaps in that direction since first starting on this journey of getting to know me. However, I know that there is more to be accomplished.

Now, instead of ignoring what it is trying to tell me, I listen and am, at times, amazed at just how simple and gratifying it is to pinpoint the problem and handle it. The physical body will respond willingly to tender, loving care. It can and will heal itself in record time with our help. The more we respect and communicate with it, the higher its vibration becomes, thus working toward the same goal of mastership.

I received this channeling from Kuthumi not too long ago. He is a Master of high vibration, who has walked embodied on Planet Earth. This is what he told me:

The bodies I will address at this time are the Etheric, Mental and Physical. The first two are not of this world, Earth. They are always a part of you, the Spirit/Soul—have always been and shall always be.

However, the physical or material body is not. I will liken it unto a house that you have chosen to live in. It can be beautiful, loved and is also a living organism, capable of feelings. When you decide to change location, you do not consider taking your house with you. It would be far too difficult to do so.

So you move on, leaving your beautiful, well-cared-for house, or it could be the opposite—a run down, falling apart, in shambles house—unloved and uncared for. If it be the latter, you then are only too willing to say good-bye and good riddance.

Meanwhile, you, with your beautiful, ever young Mental and Etheric bodies, with all the attributes of the Physical but without those earthly properties of disease, aging and so forth which the physical body is subject to, move on to find a new, more suitable home in which to dwell.

There will, however, come a time—and it is getting close—when the Physical body will take on the lighter, more radiant aspect of the Etheric. A well-cared-for house will maintain its beauty and youth through the loving care of its owner.

Likewise, the Physical body will retain its reflection of the Etheric's ever-youthful appearance. It will become more alive, more beautiful, younger in appearance and will discard any of the old baggage it has been carrying around—all of the past trauma and pain.

So whatever your belief system is regarding your ascension, be it in this lifetime or another, take care of your physical body. Visualize it growing lighter, vibrating at a higher frequency. The closer you can bring your Physical body into the higher vibration of your Etheric and Mental bodies, the closer you will be to ascension.

When the Physical has been cleared of all its past accrual of negativity, the ascension will take place. Or, to put it another way, when all of your bodies are vibrating in synchronicity with each other at the high frequency of Spirit, you then will have the ability to dematerialize and materialize when and wherever you wish.

Wishing you the Mastership of Ascension, I AM KUTHUMI.

Now that, to me, would be real Mastership. I've made great progress this lifetime on my way to the Light. However, I guess I'll have to admit that, as yet, I haven't achieved that high of a vibration—at least not within all of my bodies. Heck, I can't even levitate—yet.

Oh well, life is great and each day walks me into new experiences, bringing me ever closer to that moment. I'm really in no hurry. After all, an eternity doesn't seem nearly as long as it used to. That's because I am always in the NOW, thus there is neither tomorrow nor yesterday.

Materialize—dematerialize. Maybe mañana—who knows? I trust that I will be able to do both. However, until I get my full mastership, I better let well enough alone. Otherwise I might find myself in a rather awkward position scattered here, there and everywhere.

So until then, I'll continue doing what I enjoy, allowing life to flow as I ride on the wings of Unconditional Love.

You cannot love and fear at the same time—

it is impossible

for

LOVE FREES YOU

Fear traps you

MAINTAINING ONE'S SANITY

IN AN INSANE WORLD

All the world's a stage on which we came to play
Now we can't remember who we are
or why we came this way

Many of us, these days, appear to be out of step not only with others, but with ourselves as well. Some may judge this as insane, not normal—but really, what is normal, and what isn't? I don't know, do you? The answer always lies in whose viewpoint we are viewing it from. Believe me, this is important for each of us to remember—there is more than one's own viewpoint, and we each have the right to our own.

The Universe must maintain its balance at all times, or it would destroy itself. This is also true of our own individual universe. When we get too far out of balance, we then begin creating destruction and havoc.

There is power in unity. However, the insanity of the Illusion will eventually create a separation within, thus diminishing our power, unless we use our awareness by taking responsibility. The reflection of not being in our own balance will also affect those around us, creating more separation and judgment.

This phenomenon is throwing all of us off balance as we become caught up in war and hatred, which seems to be an almost ever day occurrence. That reflection is also bringing to the surface our own anger and pain, creating thoughts and actions of retaliation. It is our fears of what will happen in the future along with what we have experienced and judged in the past, that fans the flames of war, hatred and retaliation.

Being out of balance within our own universe will also throw us out of balance with the great Universal Mind. It also keeps us from being in the moment—we jump from past to future with our "what ifs" of judgment and fears.

A wonderful scenario was depicted in the movie A Beautiful Mind. It was a fascinating example of how one can create the phenomenon known as schizophrenia, through the separation of the goddess or feminine—the creative part, and the god or masculine—the logical part. Both of these reside within each of us, as does the child.

From what I have observed on my path, the feminine, or goddess within, begins to create that which possesses no real or tangible qualities as far as other people are concerned.

This will then create a separation between her and the logical masculine side, walling off communication between the two. The masculine is the manifestor, and he, due to the separation, will no longer be able to communicate with her in order to keep a balance of what is being created and manifested.

When this occurs, that which we know as reality will then no longer be a part of her world. Thus she continues creating scenarios that seem unreal to those who are involved, and are observing the actions of that person. They only see the outward appearance, not the separation and the imbalance manifesting within the god/goddess.

If this phenomenon is allowed to continue, the person moves further and further into his/her new reality. Then he/she is unable to return to "the real world." Thus the goddess, or feminine part of the triangle—male, female, child—continues creating that which is now her own world of reality, separate from everyone else's. The imbalance eventually becomes so predominant that it sends the whole unit—the person—into what may lead to destruction of self and sometimes others as well.

Each of us creates new or parallel worlds for ourselves in our daydreams and imagination. They become our own little fantasy worlds for escape and pleasure. However, we stay in control. Thus the god/goddess is not separated, and so our logical side keeps all in balance.

However, if one allows oneself to play too long in one's "fantasy world," that person may begin creating a world of their own, more acceptable to the goddess. Then the entire unit will move closer into their new world, and out of the one we call reality. If the goddess can't get back into balance, she may then begin creating scenarios of self—destruction with the assistance of fear driving her further over the edge.

The person will then react by doing irrational and unconventional things, reflecting the imbalance within. This is when loved ones or close friends usually step into the picture, and try to put an end to what they term as insane acts.

By this time the situation has gotten pretty well out of hand. The person is then turned over to psychiatrists, who usually resort to such outrageous practices as shock treatments and drugs. These barbaric treatments will stop the goddess in her tracks, creating a sort of comatose reaction. It will also create a sort of lethargic stupor in the logical masculine side, which turns the person into a "vegetable," unable to think or act for self.

Since the separation still exists, there can be no real healing or progress for the person. They then become, more or less, a part of what is known as the living dead. Our insane asylums are filled to over capacity with those who can no longer function in this world.

The man portrayed in this movie did, however, choose to take his power back. He reclaimed his life by balancing his god/goddess within, saying no to all who looked upon him as a victim. He also got a handle on those in his fantasy world, turning them off and tuning them out. In other words, he faced his demons, head on, and defeated them, becoming a Nobel Prize winner in place of a blithering idiot.

My point in this is to show that there are alternative ways to bring balance to self. When we do, then we are more able to assists others who are on the edge of joining in this insane game that is being dramatized on Planet Earth at this time.

Much is happening in both polarities, some of which is assisting the Mother and her children. However, with fear, distrust, judgment and retaliation going on, it may look as though everyone is spinning out, and that the whole world is becoming insane.

Mother Earth is also reacting to this through volcanoes, drought, hurricanes, and earthquakes, and is really shaking things up on her own. This, of course, only adds to the already overload we each are struggling with.

What will it take, I wonder, to get Earth's children to see what they are creating through their fears, hatred and actions of retaliation? When and how will it all end? From what I have seen and been told, when we all unite, creating love and peace instead of fear and hatred with our judgments. This is when we will achieve that for which we all strive— love and peace, individually and collectively.

I was given this poem some time ago, which is, as the saying goes, more truth than poetry. When it first started coming to me, I didn't like what it was saying so balked at writing it down. However, Spirit was insistent—very insistent. Then when I got it written, I saw the real message and why Spirit was so insistent.

I entitled it WHEN WE ALL GET ON LINE, which in one sense means 'come together.' Here it is:

Out of the shadows of the valley of fright walks the night
Down from the sky pours torrential rain driving us insane
Bombs exploding listen to the cry of the wounded, just before they die
And we may even get a message that the big A's on its way
Now that, I'm certain, would really make our day
But everything will be just fine when we all get on line

Ice caps melting but it's going to be all right
As water rises to the max, covering everything in sight
Just listen to the sizzle of volcano's liquid fire
Turning everything to ash, just like a funeral pyre
But let us all be happy, let us all be gay
Never mind those tornadoes sweeping all we own away
For everything will be just fine when we all get on line

Of course, that is a big order, because within Illusion's negative experience lies separation and judgment. However, more and more are returning to the truth—becoming aware that they no longer need to experience those negative "vibes."

Rising above the darkness of judgments and negative thoughts raises ones vibration into the realm of love and understanding. When this occurs, then even that which we have labeled as Evil takes on a different aspect of itself.

The word "Evil" has been the prime subject for some time and, at times, has been misused by labeling that which we do not like or understand as evil. Since I had no conception of exactly what is or is not Evil, I started getting the itch to explore that which I did not understand and, being limited in my own knowledge, called upon The Spirit of Enlightenment. This is what I was told:

It is through the choice of Free Will that the emotions of love and joy, or hate and judgment are explored within the vast concept of THE ALL THAT IS.

Through the primal urge to survive and misguided understanding of this phenomenon, some chose to experience the lower vibrations of fear and judgment for reflection and understanding. This was to allow one their choice of path. However, as the Illusion became more dense, the ability to remember the reason of just why that path was chosen became less and less. Thus the true path of love and light became distorted.

The emotion known as pleasure then became a two-edged sword, used in both polarities—the Light and The Dark of the Light—both in the name of love. However, since the Dark's perception of Love has been considerably distorted, they have become trapped within those low vibrations.

Wanting to be of service in some way and still containing a vague yet distorted conception of what Love is, some have endeavored to seek pleasure through acts of what might be termed as evil. And, in doing so, believe that they are doing it out of love.

Since all of this misconception stems from their own pain, hatred, and judgment, it has developed into what one might call evil creations. This has, of course, snowballed, becoming unfathomable to the ones who have either experienced that lower side of pleasure and refuse to view it as part of their creation, or who refused to go there in the first place.

Thus, judgment, fear, anger and thoughts of retaliation come into play, for who doesn't fear Evil? Even the word, itself, makes one shudder from fear and memories of other scenarios hidden deep within.

Love begets love and Fear begets fear, each expanding itself in its own way. Both reflect their separate viewpoints, thus either lowering or raising the vibration—LOVE FREES YOU. FEAR TRAPS YOU.

Thus, when one judges something as evil, it will immediately lower their vibration and will put them in harm's way of that energy. However, one should be very wary of labeling that which they do not understand, for the bottom line is the judgment one places upon something.

Judgment is brought on by fear—fear of not surviving, and there is no such thing as not surviving for we are eternal Spirit. So when judgment is removed, then Fear has no power. This will then restore the true vibration of Love where joyous pleasure abounds in its true light.

The only way Fear and Evil can have any control over anyone is to go into agreement with it. This will then enhance the power of those low vibrations.

When Lord Jesus said GET THEE BEHIND ME, SATAN, He was saying that He knew where those kinds of thoughts could lead, and refused to have any part of them. However, if one feels more comfortable in their company, then they still have more to experience and walk through.

Yes, there is Evil and we are all capable of creating and experiencing it, and most of us have at one time or another. However, by understanding this phenomenon, we can then feel compassion and love without judging. Then any hold it may try to claim it has on us will have no power—no effect.

When we no longer have the need to experience pleasure from

joining in those lower games of negativity, is when we begin playing in the high court of love and light.

The insanity of war is created from fear brought on by judgment. Ego has a big part in this, for whatever it doesn't understand it wants to control or destroy, thus receiving pleasure from those low vibrations

Many of our so called leaders talk about love while dropping bombs on their fellow man, insisting that their viewpoint is right and the other is wrong. I, for one, know that you can't expect love to be returned for bombs and control.

I liken war to the story of the person who had two little puppies, and decided to see what they would do if he rubbed their noses together. So he did, and the puppies reacted by attacking each other, never realizing that someone else was creating the anger and pain.

Perhaps we should take a look at who really is rubbing our noses together creating war and hate, and the reason behind it. Could it be that some, in the name of love, have an ulterior motive of greed and control? Ego does play funny tricks with the mind, when it is unbalanced.

Why is there so much insanity on Planet Earth? In my humble opinion, it is as I was shown while in Germany—the false god of the Illusion, and us buying into that belief system.

There have been so many misguided religious beliefs given out by the many and varied religions, each one proclaiming to be the true and only God messenger. Here is one I heard a doctor expounding on: He was talking about the insanity of circumcising baby boys. He said that operation causes numbness at the end of the penis—the most sensitive part of that organ. They never, according to him, regain much feeling in that area again. This, of course, has been a religious practice handed down through the ages.

He asked the question, "If God wanted that part removed, why did He put it there in the first place?" This is only one example of perpetuating a misunderstanding of The Great I AM and following, without question, that misconception. There are, of course, countless examples, some of which pits brother against brother.

Due to the pull of negative and positive polarities on Planet Earth, one has to be very astute in maintaining one's own balance, or they may find themselves reacting insanely to the scenario they are experiencing. I have many times.

There are many low-vibrational people who will, if allowed, feed off of those who are of a higher vibration. They are the so-called vampires, but not the blood sucking kind portrayed in horror movies. They will, however, siphon off our life energy force without so much as a thank you. It isn't that they are evil—for them it's survival.

I've had this happen to me more than once, until I wised up. Now I'm aware that when I am around someone who seems to be talking incessantly about anything or nothing, I then may start feeling tired and disoriented. This will be a signal to me that one has entered my energy field and is draining me of energy. This will really throw one into a spin.

Low-vibrational people can really do a number on those whose vibration is high, if allowed. Thus it is up to each of us to take responsibility, and remove ourselves from their clutches immediately.

As one climbs the scale from unawareness to awareness, we will then do whatever it takes to protect self. This is not "being selfish." However, if we do otherwise by not taking responsibility of protecting ourselves—i.e. putting ourself first—we then become *selfless*. I'm very certain that is not what God wants of any of us, for how then could we be that magnificent Being's reflection?

Since I have learned to love myself, unconditionally, it has been easy to put myself first. Upon doing this, I now take total responsibility for myself and my actions. Thus I never put myself in harm's way, unless I so choose for experience.

This has been another misconception of love. According to the old teachings, one is supposed to always put self last, which, of course, creates a deflated ego, not a balanced one. When one becomes a doormat for others, they usually get stepped on, and can really feel abused. This creates the feeling of being a victim, blaming others for our misfortune, thus lowering our own vibration.

I have played some pretty nutty games in my life by not taking responsibility for myself. One such incident was when I allowed others to sweet talk me out of my life savings. This happened while living in California.

I had gathered a nice little "nest egg" from the sale of my home and some money Mother had left me. Then I got greedy, and wanted more. I then proceeded to attract some whose ethics left much to be desired. You know the old saying "there's a sucker born every minute and two to take him." Evidently I was wearing a big flashing neon sign reading, "I'm a sucker, with money—come and get it." And they did.

Of course, Ego played a big part in this scenario. It made me feel "so-o-o very special" to have such important, money-affluent people paying so much attention to "little old me". I was presented with all kinds of get-rich quick schemes. Thinking that soon I would be as rich as Midas, I invested. I never stopped to observe, or even let myself think that there could be a downside. My motto was "let the games begin," and I played them all.

So my money flew out the window, along with all of those silver-tongued people whom I trusted. Finally, after realizing that my nest egg was not going to hatch, I turned off my "sucker" sign. With my credit cards maxed, and only my pension to live on, I had to resort to bankruptcy.

"Why?" I asked. "Why did this happen? I thought that if I trusted, everything would be O.K." This is when I received this very important message from MeAmba *"Child, when are you going to learn? Trusting is wonderful. However, you must be more observant, using discernment—trust only those who are trustworthy."*

After getting that bit of important advice, I then remembered that I, before investing, had the thought, "Should I do this, are they con-artists?" However, Ego came back real strong, pooh-poohing that thought, so I immediately discarded the warning and ended up broke. I did learn a very valuable lesson from the experience—to observe with discernment before leaping into the void, and to always ask for guidance, when in doubt.

I have been given some highly workable tools to assist me in maintaining my balance. Spirit does provide that which is needed to assist and protect us as we walk our path. One came to me while reading the book *Bringers of the Dawn*. It was giving information on how spinning 33 times, clockwise, would spin one out of the negative vibrations of the Mass Consciousness

"Hey, that's pretty neat," I thought, and continued reading, but not for long. Suddenly, I got a sort of jolt and heard one of my guides say, "It's more than just neat—it's a fact. However, it will do nothing for you unless you get up off of your fanny and put it to use." This I did and, with the help of my guide, began doing it. I have continued using it ever since—it really does work, but only if you use it.

This was the way I was instructed to use this tool:

Stand facing a window or something you can identify with as you complete the spin. Thus, you can keep count of how many times you have spun. While spinning, keep your eyes on your thumb(s)—you can either hold your left hand in front of you or put both thumbs together. I use the first and extend my right arm sidewise and a little toward my back, acting like a rudder.

Spin 33 times, clockwise—never counter clockwise. Clockwise spins you away from the Mass Consciousness. Counter clockwise will spin you further into it.

As I spin, with intention, I can feel the negative energies flying off of me—anger, sadness—whatever I have collected from that negative source. I am also aware of becoming lighter.

The Light is always a magnet for the negative, and spinning will release it from you. After the 33 spins, I stand with my hands over my solar plexus, and am aware that I am a little ahead of the heaviness of the Mass Consciousness. This is a wonderful tool and has served me well in keeping my vibration high and myself within my own balance.

Since we live in a physical world, in physical bodies, the action— the doing—will achieve the desired result. At least, it does for me. I presume that once we achieve Mastership, then the thought will suffice. However, until that happens, I will continue working in the physical along with Spirit. Thus achieving my goals. It's sort of like the old saying, *If you are going to pray for potatoes, you'd better grab a hoe.*

With so much insanity being dramatized on the planet at this time, I asked for words that would assist all Earth's children in staying above the low vibrations of negativity and judgment. I then received this message.

My beloved Children: I am Lord Jesus and this is my message to you:
Let go of your fears, forgive and hold no animosity toward no one,
including yourself.

Concern yourself not about your future.
Focus upon the moment that you are in.
Trust and love, unconditionally.
Allow with love, not judgment, the unfoldment of all.
Create not scarcity through your fear of lack of.
Vibrate in the high energy of the ALL THAT IS.
Look upon the Illusion for what it is—illus ion,
and behold the awesome truth of
God's Divine Plan.
For I say unto you that when you do, you will understand and
with understanding you shall be free

Always be aware

of what you put out to the Universe

for it

will be returned to you
in like manner

CONNECTING WITH GOD

We are all seekers, in one way or another, for proof of what we believe or have been told to believe—that God really does exist. That somewhere out there is a Protector with such great powers that nothing can prevail against It.

I remember Bashar telling us that we, on Planet Earth, all have this phenomenon of believing that a Greater Power does exist, not within, but outside of ourselves. It is my knowingness that this is due to heavy programming, lowering our awareness of the Truth of who we really are—a part of, not separate from, that great Source.

However, Bashar's people, unlike us, seem to have the knowingness that there is no separation between that Power and themselves. This creates a oneness that unites each, and every one of them, to the other. Thus there are no wars, no crime, nor any of the other negative aspects, which are so predominant here.

They know that each one is a vital part of the other. Thus any violent act against their brother is also a violent act against themselves.

They have worked through all of the illusion of separation, and are of one mind—one purpose, which is of being of service to self, and to others. Thus they serve the Light out of love, not fear.

Just Who, Where, What is this Powerful Energy we call God? Where does It reside? What does It really look like? Some see It as being masculine in gender, while others see It as both feminine and masculine, but always not part of, but separate from themselves.

Some see It as controlling, vengeful, and judgmental, filling the heart with fear of not obeying. Others see It as loving, compassionate, understanding, thus anything that is of the negative belongs to "the devil"—a separate entity not of the Great I AM.

Greek mythology, as well as many others, separated God into many powerful gods of questionable integrity. Each god possessed great powers, but were always somewhere else, creating a separation between God and man

What do we really see when we think of God? Is It something so awesome that we don't dare look directly upon It, believing we are not worthy, and will surely be consumed by that energy? Does that High Deity ever show Its face to mere mortals like us, or is It only available to those who are the so called "chosen ones?" And, most important of all, do we really feel we deserve to be a part of that mysterious and awesome Being?

How do I separate the myth from the truth of the one we call God—or is all of this a part of the Cosmic Joke? Having walked through the maze of many lifetimes, I remember seeing and being with many, whose loving and beautiful energy made me feel that somehow there was a connection of oneness. That their vibration was compatible to mine, giving me a wonderful feeling of wholeness.

A few years back I was alone, preparing to do an Awakening. Suddenly these words, along with the music, came to me and I began singing:

> Come now to the table, Masters of the Light
> We are your lost children, lost within our fright
> Father/Mother God, creator of all life
> We're feeling so abandoned, within this earthly strife

*LISTEN, OH, MY CHILDREN! LOOK AND YOU WILL SEE
THE NEW WORLD THAT IS DAWNING IN LOVE AND
   HARMONY
CHILD, I'D NEVER LEAVE YOU, I'M NOT IN HEAVEN ABOVE
BUT WALKING CLOSE BESIDE YOU IN ETERNAL LOVE*

Thank you, oh my God, for now I truly see,
it wasn't you who left I abandoned me

*CHILD, HOW COULD I LEAVE YOU? FOR HEAVEN'S NOT
   ABOVE
TOGETHER WE CREATE IT WITH OUR ETERNAL LOVE*

These words, for me, had such a beautiful, true ring to them that I knew they were not from any of the low vibrations. I was being told that we are all a part of—not separate from—God, THE GREAT I AM, and that Heaven is, in a matter of speaking, a part of the great Myth, as is Hell.

As the words in that song said, we make our own Heaven. We also create our own hell through our actions. The higher we raise our vibration, the closer we come to our own individual heaven through our joy and, of course, the lower the vibration, the closer to our own personal hell through our fears

God, to me, is as individual as we each are. He/She/It has the power to be all things as The Great I AM. Whenever I feel that God is showering love and joy around and through me, is that not my own God-Self blending with that awesome, loving Energy?

God is the source of all energy—thus is everywhere. It can appear anywhere, at any time, in any form It so chooses, in order to connect with our own awareness. It is a shape-shifter in the truest sense of the word. This Energy is LOVE, personified and magnified, reflecting to us the message that we are a part of that powerful, loving Energy, and all we have to do is to blend with it.

Many a time I have felt separated and shut off from this life-giving Energy. It was as though my feelings, along with my awareness, were being shut down—turned off. "Why am I feeling this way? Why can't I get in touch with God—who or what is blocking me?" I would ask myself, always chasing after the thought that someone out there was throwing a "monkey-wrench" into my connection to God, thus deterring me from feeling that protective Force.

I didn't like those feelings—none of us do, for it does bring up our abandonment issues. So like so many of us, I always went searching for the culprit outside of myself, thus never receiving a true and lasting answer. When this 'shut down, turned off' feeling became too uncomfortable, I would "head for the hills" to try to shake it.

Seeking out the biggest grandfather tree around, I would wrap my arms around it, letting my body blend with its beautiful energy. Breathing deeply, I would send it my love, thanking it for being there.

Then, for some reason, a feeling of loving energy would enter my body, rejuvenating and restoring my own inner balance of love, joy and peace. After doing this, I would always have a child-like playful, energy. It was as though there had been a connection made with that powerful Being.

It took me some time to realize just why this action had such a remarkable outcome for me, giving me back that wonderful feeling of love and joy. Not only was I sending and blending my love with that big grandfather tree, I was also exchanging my energy with God 's loving energy. In other words, I was hugging God in one of Its many and varied forms.

Remember the Deer, the Red Tailed Hawks. The Golden Eagle, the "Angels" in Germany and those guiding me through that automobile accident, all making appearances when I needed them? Were they not also God in Its many and varied forms touching my own inner God Self?

And what about the touch of a friendly hand, the laughter of a child, the smell of wet grass after a summer rain, or a beautiful sunrise or sunset painting the sky with radiant colors—the list is endless, as is God's eternal love.

After viewing all of this and wondering why I, at times, was unable to connect with this awesome Source, I decided to look within and not outside of myself for my answers. I knew that God is everywhere and everything and is available to all, so It certainly wasn't blocking me, causing me to feel separated and shut down.

"How can I contact that awesome Power at will? What did I do up on the mountain, besides hugging a tree, that brought It to me?" Sifting through my many jumbled thoughts, something came to the fore, which had a ring of truth to it—I breathed out love. That was all I did—*I breathed out Love.*

There is a Universal Truth, which is *That which you put out you will get back.* So I began to examine what I was feeling and putting out during those "shut down" times. And that was exactly it—nothing but negative, turned-off feelings. I was the culprit—it was a creation of my own, as always, which made me the victim to my own feelings.

"What can I do to handle this? If I really am not feeling nor sending out love or kind thoughts, then how can I connect with those feelings I lack?" I was on the horns of that darn dilemma again, and it wasn't very comfortable.

This is when I got this message—*FAKE IT TILL YOU MAKE IT!*

So, without further questioning or looking for other alternatives, I began breathing deeply, and with every out-breath I thought and said, "*I LOVE YOU!*" And, as if by magic, I began to feel love coming back as I breathed in.

At first it was small, almost unnoticeable. However, with every intake of breath, I felt more love, more power. I kept breathing love out and in. Then wonder of wonders, suddenly I knew without a doubt that I no longer was faking it. It was for real. *Love was, is, and always will be available to us.* All we have to do is to be open to its wonderful, healing energy.

So remember: *What you put out you get back.* It doesn't matter whether you feel love or not. Do what I did, start consciously breathing out love, saying *I love you,* and also be willing to receive it back. In other words, *fake it till you make it,* and the magic will happen. It did for me, and it will for you.

Death
is
only another way of
Spirit
experiencing itself

For all is life in its varied forms of
transformation

DEATH AND BEYOND

In my reality, there is no death—only life. The rest is illusion, thus death is also a part of life, and is just another way of Spirit experiencing itself. This was one of the many valuable lessons my son, Jimmy, taught me, while I was working through his transformation. It was also Lord Jesus' beautiful message. Thus, in my reality, I no longer look upon death the way I use to.

However, since the Illusion still holds the concept that one must die in order to "escape," I decided to explore that phenomenon and came up with this conclusion:

First I asked myself, "If death is an escape, then why am I still here?" After all, I have distinct and vivid memories of walking through many lifetimes on Planet Earth—some of which, from my viewpoint, were not the most joyful. Thus I would not really care to experience them again. Why did I keep doing so? What kept bringing me back, lifetime after lifetime?

I have proven to myself that others also return, for I have met many whom I remembered as co-creators of past-life scenarios. Some scenarios I then judged as good while others were not so palatable. This left me with not wanting to remember some, while longing to remember and even relive those that I had enjoyed.

Of course, this doesn't work. For when we try to shut out or forget the things we consider bad, wanting to remember only the good, will eventually lead to bad memory and forgetfulness> This will then keep us out of being completely in present time.

We keep repeating our lifetimes over and over, in different and varied scenarios without the foggiest idea of what we are doing. There does, however, seem to be that little voice within whispering words of encouragement, urging us to keep on keeping on.

So, if death is not an escape, then where do we, as Spirit, go when we leave our physical body? Are we still caught in Illusion's web, and held there while we undergo the process of memory erasing? Then do we return to earth to start life anew with a new body, and no memory of what transpired in the previous one?

As I said earlier, the veil is becoming very thin, and many of us are rising above the clutches of the false god. We are remembering and disproving that death is an escape. In doing so, we also are releasing the shackles of past judgments that locked us into the Illusion's game of no escape. Once we see it for what it is, we then are free from its negative vibration.

I received a wonderful channeling concerning this from The Council of Twelve, which I will share with you. They always address me as Daughter of the Light when channeling through me. They entitled it *LIFE THE MOVIE.* This is what they said: *Greetings, Daughter of the Light:*

With each birth there is an experience of a new fragment of the whole— a new way of looking at oneself.

When death occurs, that particular fragment remains as a memory as new ex-plorations begin with each new birth. The prior memory of the old life slips into the background as the "new you" with a new body begins, once again, exploring and expanding life in new and exciting ways.

The Higher Whole Soul Self is constantly sifting through, separating "the wheat from the chaff," thus gleaning new ways to look at Itself.

Then in one certain lifetime, usually after many lifetimes spent on Planet Earth, there is an explosion of memory where all begins to come into focus.

Thus the fragments left behind start coming out of the hidden past, as memories flood into the present life that you are experiencing. They can be quite overwhelming and so must be sorted out by your Higher All-knowing Self.

Painful, judgmental lifetimes may rise up for you to recognize as fragments of yourself in order to be integrated. This allows you to recognize, and become more of who you are.

However if looked upon as, shall we say, a movie you are watching, allowing yourself to view it without judgment, it will be painless and pleasurable and highly beneficial in opening up your awareness.

You then will glean much from reliving your many lifetimes, as you allow those fragments to come together. When this integration is complete, you then become that which you truly are—not a part of the whole but all of the whole or, to put it another way, your Higher Soul Self.

You have paid for your ticket, have acted out the many parts you chose to experience, and are now remembering. So take a front-row seat and enjoy your own special movie of your very own special life.

ACTION—LIGHTS—CAMERA.—LET IT ROLL!

We leave you surrounded in our love and light.

THE COUNCIL OF 12

So since death is not the escape that many at this time believe, but only a temporary rest from physical experience, then what is? Evidently the high vibration of love and awareness is the true answer.

The judgment we heap upon ourselves lowers our vibration, keeping us buried within the concepts of the Illusion. Those who proclaim themselves as being the "messengers of God" have told us that we are all born in sin. Perhaps we are, for we do return with all of our past garbage in tow, which keeps us in Illusion's low vibration until released.

Believing that there is no way that we can rise above it makes it so. Thus, we stay within that illusion until we wake up, releasing all those negative thought forms to the Light. This is our responsibility, for whatever we create, we can un-create through awareness and love.

When we do, magical things happen. Our vibration rises, we feel lighter, more aware. We find that we are loving everyone and everything, especially ourselves, instead of judging. We then see life for what it is—an ever-flowing, ever-expanding experience into infinity.

Since everything is vibration, the higher we vibrate, the more our awareness expands. Then, when we are vibrating at a higher ratio than the Illusion, we will rise like the Phoenix Bird from the ashes of the past, and will be free to explore other dimensions of awareness.

Speaking of other dimensions my friend Jim and I were engaged in an interesting conversation over a cup of coffee regarding the Third, Fourth and Fifth Dimensions.

He had attended a Hopi Indian Powwow while in Arizona, and was telling me what they had revealed in their talks. It went something like this: When one leaves the Third Dimension, they will go into Fifth and then must either return to Fourth or go into what they termed the void.

Early the next morning I was given this clarification from Spirit: The Third Dimension is made up of physicality where negative and positive polarities exist simultaneously, for choices of exploration and experience.

The Fifth Dimension is the passageway into higher dimensions of Light and Love, of which the physical, as we know it, is no longer a part. This is due to the Fifth's high vibration.

The Fourth is still the physical without the illusion of struggle, strife and death. It is the gateway, where we can return to experience physicality without getting caught in the negative polarity or The Dark of the Light, as Archangel Michael refers to it.

This will enable those, who so choose, to return to physical after their transformation from Third to Fifth. Thus they have the awareness and ability to assist those still within the illusion of the Third Dimension without becoming trapped.

Those who no longer wish to experience the physical will use the Fifth Dimension as the gateway to higher vibrations—the Fifth being Unconditional Love. Thus they can, after experiencing that high vibration, go on to even higher realms of understanding, compassion and love. They then become lighter—more Spirit—assisting others of lesser vibration.

There are some who become such high masters of vibration that they can materialize and dematerialize at will. Thus they can appear in the physical and then vanish instantly. From what I understand, they have the ability to slow down or speed up their vibration, thus becoming visible or invisible to those of lesser awareness.

There is never an end to expanding our awareness, knowledge, and love. It is all within our reach when we are ready.

I trust that this will assist you in your understanding as it has me. Once we are able to see the whole picture instead of our one little bitty present lifetime, we then can understand ourselves, and why we are such "habitual ritualers."

That is when the murky suppressive clouds of unknowingness and unawareness give way to the golden sunshine of Truth, lifting us ever higher on our path out of the Illusion into the Light.

Until you love yourself unconditionally
without judgment
You cannot truly love

IT'S ALL ABOUT LOVE

Love is the key
Open your heart and set yourself free

Before I opened my heart to feeling I was, more or less, a lost soul—as are many people on Planet Earth wandering aimlessly through life. Like them, I was searching for my truth in order to gain some sort of balance within me.

Spirit is moving in wondrous ways and many messages are being given to us in these times. If we are closed down—not open to believing and receiving those higher messages of love and light, then we are unable to feel the protective love that is being showered upon us in these troubled times.

"The voice of freedom must be stilled," screams the suppresser—the controller. However, there is now a louder, more persistent voice. It is the voice of Love, whispering to each of us, resonating deep within. And Its whisper is becoming a thunderous roar, mighty in its message, unlocking our innermost feelings and setting us free.

The physical body, due to its density, may still feel imprisoned. However, we—the Spirit—no longer will remain slaves to those who would control. When love replaces fear, doubt, and judgment, we then will rise above Illusion's control.

I experienced how very powerful Unconditional Love really is one day while in my Awakening room. I had gone into a very deep meditation and rose into a higher realm above this third dimension. As I was returning, I could hear the beautiful music of One Love being sung. It was glorious, as though a chorus of Angels were serenading me.

Opening my eyes, I became aware that Lord Jesus and other high Masters of the Light were there, surrounding me and filling me with love. I felt so much love that there seemed to be no room for any other feeling or emotion. All negativity had been swept away, like clouds giving way to golden sunshine.

The love I felt was all encompassing, all expanding,—going wider, deeper, higher until nothing but love existed. It began filling every nook and corner of my Being.

I seemed to be expanding further and further out into Infinity. It was like looking through the eyes of God with no judgment, only love.

"So this is what love really is—no separation, only oneness," I whispered in wide-eyed wonderment. This is what we are missing here on planet Earth—that glorious feeling of oneness with neither control nor judgment. It was awesome and I didn't want to come back, to leave that beautiful space I was in.

Finally returning back into my physical body, I received this channeling on Love.

MY BELOVED CHILDREN: You have been searching for that which is and always has been with you—Love. Love is the very essence from which you came and was placed there by The Great Creator in the beginning. You have asked, "What is love? How does it feel?" And so I answer.

Love is the most powerful energy of all. It restores all life, erases all pain, and turns fear to joy. Its energy restores and makes young and whole again. Negative forces cannot prevail against it, for Love is the powerful force of The Great I AM—THE ALL THAT IS—GOD.

Within Love there is no judgment, for judgment feeds the fear, the hate, the negative and causes pestilence and famine. Fear lowers the vibrations, which then will make you subject to the so-called negative side of the picture. You cannot love and walk in judgment. You are either vibrating in the high vibration of love or the lower vibration of judgment.

There has been much talk about Love and its properties but mere words are inadequate to explain the awesomeness of Love. You must feel the vibration deep within, for it is the heartbeat, the very pulse of God, Itself.

Your very fiber—the essence of who you are—is love. It is the Nectar of which you are made. I am not talking about the body in which you reside at this time, but about you, the living Spirit made in the image of God with all of Its power, wisdom and love.

When you think of yourself in those terms, how can you not love yourself? And when you do not, then is that not an invalidation of the Supreme Being's gift of life to you? When you say, "We are not worthy," are you not then telling God that there was a mistake, and that you were created imperfect? GOD MAKES NO MISTAKES.

There has been much said about where you came from, but are they talking about you, the Spirit or the body in which you are living while incarnate? Yes, the body is made from the elements of the sea, and earth, but that does not make it impure, something to ignore, to mistreat, for it is of your beloved Mother Earth.

It serves you well and if it doesn't, it is only because you do not love it. If there is pain, listen to your body. Remember all that your body wants is to be loved and recognized, and since you are the essence of Love Itself, you have the power to heal your body.

If you believe God is perfect, then so are you, for you were made in the image of God. If you believe you are imperfect then you must also believe God also is imperfect.

Forget past teachings, they were misinterpreted by those who did not understand or wished to control. Put no judgment upon the past, it now is only an illusion. Love the moment. The old is no more. Step into the NOW—the beautiful world of Love and Light.

God placed the light of Love within you when you were created. Find that light for self. Love is your birthright. God gave it to all of His children.

You all are perfect. How could you be otherwise? You were made out of God's golden essence.

Love is the key—use it. Love your fears, your doubts, your pain and, yes, your judgments for in doing so you will set yourself free. The negative is only an illusion—Love is real. Love yourself first and the rest will fall into its proper place.

For I say unto you UNTIL YOU LOVE YOURSELF COMPLETELY, WITHOUT JUDGMENT, YOU CANNOT LOVE.

I wish you Love, Understanding and Radiant Joy
ONE IN SPIRIT   I AM LORD JESUS THE CHRIST

This message and what transpired just before it has given me a broader and more expanded view of all life, be it the past or present. I now realize that life is a fantastic play, which never ends.

The curtain, at certain times, goes down blocking my view from the changes that are being made back stage. However, that does not mean I no longer am a part of the play. The curtain does go up, and I find myself once again the star in my own reality. Others, of course, also have their own important roles to act out.

What goes on behind the curtain that blocks my view from seeing past the veil, I wonder? Perhaps I am learning to read my part differently, taking on another aspect of myself. I know of quite a few lifetimes when I have taken on the masculine role, which doesn't surprise me—after all, we are both feminine and masculine.

When we meet up with those with whom we have bonded in a loving way, the vibration will become stronger, deeper, more expanding. However, upon meeting those whom I refer to as "worthy opponents" then we sometimes react in ways not so loving.

Since there are no mistakes, and everything comes up in our face to either judge or love, then perhaps those opponents was not the devil himself. It may have been someone acting out their part in such a way as to assist us in seeing the dark side of ourselves.

Yes, I have known the devil, met it face to face many times. However, upon closer inspection, I found it was not a separate entity, but a part of me—of my belief system playing out my dark side.

It did contain all of that so-called entity's negative aspects. However, let's "give the devil its due" for those experiences did assist me in my judgments. Thus I created something I could blame for my actions, instead of taking on my own responsibility. When this occurs, it does support our misguided beliefs that we are the helpless victim, and so releases us from taking responsibility, or so we tell ourselves.

Since recognizing the power that Love truly is, and knowing how judgment can derail one from finding their truth, I now allow myself the luxury of seeing everything from a higher, more expanded awareness.

I did have to cut through layers of my social veneer in order to discover this deeply rooted truth. How long it took does not matter, for I have found whatever it takes the end results far outweighs the cost—be it time, effort, money or whatever. The end result being the prize of prizes—that dazzling brilliant light of love, which we all are and, once found, will never fade away.

I know, for I had lost my light so long ago, lost in the lies and half—truths within the murky myth of the Illusion. Having lost and now having found it again makes it my most treasured possession.

You know, my friends, I do sort of hate to burst your bubble of having someone or something outside of yourself to blame for your so-called misfortunes in life. However, the truth is that the devil, along with hell's fire, are all a part of the Cosmic Joke placed there by none other than ourselves in order to have a game to play.

Ah, what fools we mortals be, until we open our eyes and see that Love is the only key

Allow yourself to soar
Without limitation or reservation

for

there are no limitations
except those which we place upon

OURSELVES

FREE SPIRIT—RESTLESS SOUL

I hear the north wind blowing
down the valley and it's telling me
Now I must be traveling
for the snows will soon be here
So I say goodbye to all my friends
Then I hit the road again
I'm following that wild bird that I hear

I have always been what one might call "a restless soul", always searching for that one place, that certain someone or something, which would quiet my restlessness—filling the empty void lying somewhere, deep within.

Whenever I see wild geese flying, their happy honking always calls for me to follow, giving me a sort of an excited yet melancholy feeling. What wondrous adventures will they encounter on their way? Will they ever be content, or will they too feel that restless call of wanting to explore the new—the unknown?

I know that within each of us lies the powerful Master of Light, which, if allowed, will be guided and tempered by the love of the Inner Child. However, sometimes we forget that we also are the Child, thus shutting down that beautiful energy of fun-loving innocence

Come, let your imagination run free. Allow yourself to be the child, and join me in experiencing a mad cap adventure of what may appear to be the "never-never land of enchantment." The child in you will love it. Then when you feel its happiness bubbling up inside of you, you will also be happy. So together let us explore the exciting world of our Inner Child, letting our imagination run free.

The thrill of adventure is strong in most of us—the wild beat of a jungle drum, the cry of a wolf on a winter night, the wonderment of what might be just over that next mountain, or around the next bend.

Perhaps a space ship is hiding in a cloud, just above us, or a Big Foot lurking in the trees. Yes, the mysteries of the unknown can set the heart pounding, stirring up unfathomable emotions lying dormant within us. All of these I have experience, not in my imagination but in the physical. For as Bashar always said *"Believing is seeing—not the other way around."*

Once we break through the barriers of being limited, we then become aware that there is much more out there waiting to meet the eye in the physical than we could possibly imagine in our wildest imagination. It is only our buying into the Mass Consciousness of limitation that keeps us blinded to what is out there in the *real world.*

As the Masters have always told us "there are worlds without end." They remain in other dimensions, other parallel worlds, waiting for us to raise our awareness to a higher vibration of love. When we do, they will make themselves known. They did for me, and they will for you. However, if we are fearful of what we will encounter, that lowers our vibration, and they remain invisible. It all has to do with the "vibes" we are putting out—Love or Fear.

Have you ever watched cloud formations? Let your inner child guide you. One minute you will see a poodle, then a sheep, or a dragon blowing it's fiery breath as the sun's rays catches it just right. Like life, they are always forming and reforming themselves into all kinds of shapes. All one has to do is to let their child-like imagination come forth as the storybook unfolds. As Archangel Michael said, *You can experience a lot by watching clouds.*

So why not allow yourself to remember that you are also a child. Then the world will once again become new and unexplored. I allow myself the fun of doing this. In fact, I sometimes allow the child in me to feel free, unencumbered, knowing that magical things are happening. And, when I do, wonderful, magical things do happen.

Sitting by a little mountain stream, 1 hear it calling to the child in me to come and play. If I don't become stuck in the Mass Consciousness concept that I cannot be a child, I find myself becoming a part of that little stream as it happily gurgles around rocks, splashing itself towards its destination.

Since we are all things, let us once more be the child, enjoying life through its eyes. Perhaps if we would allow ourselves more freedom of Being, there wouldn't be so much hatred and anger on the planet.

I am as free and as happy as I allow myself to be.

However, sometimes I forget to allow myself that freedom, and I am sure you do too. When this happens, life becomes a drag. This is when I start buying into the concepts of the Mass Consciousness limitations. Believe me, it is not a very pleasant feeling, especially once you have tasted the joys of being a free spirit.

Perhaps our restlessness stems from long-ago memories begging to be remembered. Could it be that before we allowed our awareness strands of DNA to be shut down, we could experience whatever we so chose—to run with the wolf, or be a panther silently stalking its prey?

We might even have that close encounter with one of our Space Brothers, or sit on a mountainside and communicate with a Big Foot? Since God is THE ALL THAT IS, and we are a part of that glorious Being, then it stands to reason that we are connected to everything, great and small. I sometimes feel that way. Do you?

The more I explore the possibilities of what life has to offer, the more excited I become. This is when the concept of the oneness of all things becomes real to me, challenging me to explore, to open up, to raise my awareness above what I have been told is truth. When all we have are other people's concepts of life, it certainly limits our own perception.

Their truth is valid. However, mine is for me just as valid, as should yours be for you. I am as entitled to mine as they are to theirs.

We are all part of the Living Library. Thus, when we allow ourselves to share this wonderful treasure of the pure truth, it becomes a shining beacon of light lifting our awareness higher and higher into what really exists here and elsewhere.

I know that as I rise to higher levels of awareness more is opening up for me to access and explore. I also know that it is opening up for you, as well. All you have to do is to be aware that it is. Everything is contained within the ALL THAT IS—by definition it can not be otherwise. So since we are a part of that great wealth of knowledge of love and light, perhaps all we have to do is to step out of our doubts and our fears, allowing ourselves to step through that door.

The excitement we feel is the child calling to us to set ourselves free. One of the teachings I learned from Bashar was this: *Excitement and fear are the exact same feeling, until judged.* So why not "go for the gusto" and choose excitement?

"Seek and ye shall find. Knock and it shall be opened unto you" were gems of truth told to us so long ago. However, we didn't allow ourselves to shake off the bonds of limitation, and so they became just words.

There are worlds without end for us to explore to our heart's content—nothing is impossible. Only our own concepts of our limitations make it so, along with our fears of what we may encounter and/or what others think. Until we shake off the bonds of judgment completely, and allow ourselves to truly be who we are, these thoughts will set us into self-doubting, closing us off to wondrous adventures of exploration and fulfillment.

No longer am I fearful of what I may encounter, whether it be on the other side of those closed doors of my memory, or whatever the future may bring. Furthermore, I no longer give a hoot what others think of me. Love erases all fear—love for myself and whatever lies around the next bend or over the next hill. Whatever I have chosen to experience, I am willing to face with no judgment, no incrimination. Thus there is nothing to fear as I open another door to the many faceted, yet unexplored me.

Isn't it time you do the same for you?

There is nothing that we
as individuals
or
as a conscious group
cannot achieve

PAST—PRESENT—FUTURE

We have, my friends, walked many paths, experienced many things and, although it may have appeared to be otherwise at times, we were never alone.

I often thought that I was the only one climbing that long winding road with its sharp curves and steep grades filled with fear, pain and loneliness. Now, I know differently. It was only the Illusion that kept me from seeing that we each were a part of the plan, sharing and assisting each other on our journey to enlightenment.

Many times, like you, I thought I had reached the top. However, stretching out before me would be even higher, more expansive heights to scale. In comparison, the ones I had conquered appeared no larger than foothills. Thus, each became a gradient step for my evolution of what was to follow, making me stronger, more determined to complete my journey.

Sometimes I felt that my struggle was over. However, soon I would find myself again on a path leading back down into shadowy illusions of pain, fear and judgment. Eventually the path would lead me out of that dark valley, and once again I would be climbing to new heights of awareness.

Of course, there were always those wonderful times of just allowing myself to relax, be happy, accepting life as it unfolded. These were the times devoted to the child essence, which are so very necessary for our well being.

However, after a while, there would come that feeling of urgency to "get on with the program." Then, once again, I'd find myself tearing away at the fabric of the Illusion with intent and bulldog tenaciousness.

Deep down, most of us have the feeling that time is a lie. That one day our beautiful Mother Earth will rise up and become the glorious star she is destined to be.

The past became less and less traumatic, as I let go of my dramatizations and judgments. The present lifetime began taking on a new luster with deeper understanding, compassion and awareness. The answers of why I, for so long, determinedly struggled on and on became very clear.

With the releasing of my judgments, fears and negative reactions to life love, along with compassion and joy, began expanding within. When this occurs within each of us, then the vibration of Mother Earth, as well as all of Her children, will also expand to a higher realm. Many of us are now coming together in trust and harmony.

At times it has seemed as though my progress has been very minute, almost undetectable. However, the fabric of the Illusion is beginning to tear apart. As the Light of Awareness and Compassion starts penetrating the dark, Love replaces fear and Illusion's negative energies.

Where will that leave us if there are no games to play, no negative energies to go forth and battle? Perhaps some of you are thinking that if there is going to be nothing to do but stand around singing hallelujahs all day, then where is the spice of life—the excitement?

Upon asking Bashar, our space brother, about this, his answer was that we have only seen the tip of the iceberg. That this was only the beginning, for out in space there are many planets whose inhabitants are in as bad or worse shape than our own.

Many Masters have said that there are other worlds of which we know nothing about. They, too, need to be raised out of their unawareness state into higher vibrations of understanding and love. They are not victims but, because of their low vibration and unawareness, they believe they are.

Those who so choose will find themselves embarking on exciting and fulfilling missions of gigantic proportions. Having been through the fray on Planet Earth, we have learned. Thus we will not go unprepared, but will go as Masters in our awareness, within the invincible armor of our love, knowledge and compassion. Our training on Planet Earth has been indispensable, giving us the tools we will need for this important mission—never again to be caught in Illusion's negative trap.

Of course, some will choose to stay on Mother Earth, enjoying Her beauty, and assisting Her in raising Her vibration even higher.

There are no limits as to what we, as individuals or as a collective group consciousness, can achieve. In the future, limitation will not be within our reality. Of one thing I am certain, lessons are being learned and graduation day is at hand. Self-realization is replacing unawareness and victimhood. We are returning to God's Golden River of Unconditional Love.

*Accept
both
Criticism and Praise
Graciously without
Judgment*

REFLECTIONS

I look in the mirror and I see
A friend smiling at me

Reflecting back over what I have experienced in this and past lives, I began recalling the judgments that I had placed upon those experiences, and how they had left me so very fragmented. However, as The Council of Twelve told me in their channeling of *Life the Movie,* this was the lifetime for me to remember, and to bring them forth. Thus I have been able to reclaim those fragmented parts and so am no longer separated from myself.

Since bringing those memories into my present reality, I now have risen above the myth that I had bought into for so long. This has given me the freedom I had only dreamed of having.

Now that all doors, which I have been made aware of, are wide open and the judgment removed, I can look at myself in the mirror without doubt or fear. In other words, I am no longer scattered to hell and back, separating myself from me and my knowingness of who I truly am. Thus I have no reason to hide from either myself or my fellow man in fear of what will happen if my "dastardly deeds" are brought out in the open for everyone to see. Ah, what sweet freedom that is—try it, you'll like it.

My "dark side" has served me well, as has yours. My son always said—*"take the judgment off. It's perfect just the way it is."* As far as I am concerned, no truer words were ever spoken, and I thank him from the bottom of my heart for teaching me that truth.

This simple truth has really set me free to love and enjoy life in whatever way it unfolds. It also has enabled me to become a Master of the Awakenings. Were I still walking in judgment, I would not be able to be effective in counseling and releasing their negative "stuff." In other words, my and their "stuff" would become one big tangled ball of negative judgments. Then no one would benefit.

Lord Jesus said it so beautifully when he said *"Remove the mote from thine own eye so you can see more clearly the mote in thy brother's.* Otherwise, if we don't remove and clear up our judgments that we have placed upon ourselves and on others, I am certain that we will not be very effective in raising our or anyone's vibration.

Walking through and out of the Illusion has been, for me, "the eye-opener of all eye openers." In other words, it is my belief that this is our ultimate goal here on Planet Earth—to see the Illusion for what it is, and to free ourselves from the entrapment of its low vibration.

Sometimes, when a past judged deed would rise up to be released, I wanted to run away and hide—to slam shut and tightly lock that door to my memory of those times, which I had created and then judged myself and others for creating them. I didn't look upon them as learning experiences, but dastardly deeds I had done to others or had allowed them to be done to me. So the real lesson of why I created them was never learned.

This is always the bottom line—*it isn't what others have done to us, but what we have done to others, or have allowed others to do to us.* This, of course, always ends up being what we have done to ourselves—The Law of One. Upon coming to that realization, we then are learning to take responsibility for our action. This is when we stop putting others or ourselves in harm's way, and become the true Masters that we are.

Yes, there was many a time I wanted to run away from realizing that whatever scenario I had either created or co-created was my responsibility. However, I know now that I would not have been there, if I weren't to experience it. Whenever I did run, guess who was waiting for me—me with all of my judgmental thought.

However, finally "came the dawn,"—the reality that sooner or later I had to own up to, and take responsibility for all of my past scenarios. So now I no longer run away, and hide from myself. Instead I go deep into the scenario, and handle it by removing all judgment. If I find this isn't working, I then call upon someone of equal or higher understanding and vibration to assist in releasing me from my own special cross, which I was creating with my judgments, anger, and fear.

Just recently I found myself becoming involved again in a scenario that I had glimpsed as a child this lifetime. I had felt that I had completely released my judgments of that scenario. However, from all appearance, there still was more work to do. There seemed to be, from what I was viewing, a very large rift between the god/goddess and child within.

I then became aware that the split was a reflection of what the Mass Consciousness was creating within The Mother's children. The Mass Consciousness can be very powerful. It can also become very destructive, when not within its balance—which it seldom, if ever, is. This is when judgment and ego rules, and the consequences are seldom pleasant to experience. They can result in catastrophic repercussions of war, hatred, fear and all those other negative illusions we are experiencing today.

Looking back over other lifetimes, I felt a sort of helpless, hopeless feeling. I saw how the Mass Consciousness was creating the same scenario of hatred, fear and war, as it had time and time again. Thus it was creating separation in many different and varied reflections on Planet Earth, causing more hatred, with thoughts of "getting even"—of retaliation and blame.

"Where is the Love? Where is the Light?" Is there ever going to be peace and joy on this beautiful Planet?" Then I remembered these words to a song. *Let there be peace on earth and let it begin with me.*

I knew that Spirit was telling me that there was work to be done within my own universe. That to become angry and judgmental would only add fuel to the fires of those negative energies, which were erupting all over the Planet. I was here to hold the Light not to detract from it with my negative thoughts and actions.

Meantime, over 200 miles from where I reside, my good friend, Jim Solo, was also feeling those negative vibes of the Illusion and called me. After an hour or more of trying to figure out what we should do, Spirit came in strong, assisting us in deciding that we should get together. Jim agreed to come to my place.

While awaiting his arrival, I washed and sunned the crystals and made the Awakening room ready. We both knew that whatever we were going to do would not only affect us greatly, but would also have rippling repercussions on Mother Earth's children as well.

Awakenings always do because, as we raise our vibrations, it will also benefit those around us creating the domino effect. This eventually will also raise the vibration of the Mass Consciousness—as more walk within the Light of Awareness, more will automatically follow.

As I worked, my mind began reflecting back to different scenarios that I had either created or co-created, then judged lowering my vibration. This then caused me to create even more negative scenarios in order to avoid looking at the Core Issue.

The Core Issue is always the big one, which has had a very long lasting effect on how we react to life today, even though it occurred in a long ago past lifetime. It is the one we have created, and because of the judgment and trauma it carries we don't want to look at or take responsibility for our part in its creation.

It's much easier to blame others for the dilemma we find ourselves in, than to take responsibility. Thus we continue either creating or co-creating lessor scenarios of trauma and pain for ourselves. We usually do this without knowing why.

It is a sub-conscious thought or judgment buried deep within our memory banks, trying to be brought to the surface in order to be recognized and released. So we continue putting ourselves in harm's way with so-called accidents, or other scenarios of pain, suffering, and failure of lessor impact than our core issue.

Since the core issue is always a scenario that we have judged, and then buried deep within our memory, it is a hard one to face. Thus we resort to using our escape mechanism by hiding from the possibility that we might be the culprit who has either created or co-created those scenarios. Trying to forget will result in bad memory and poor judgment. It also contributes in making ourselves the "whipping-boy" in life instead of being the Masters that we are.

All of these negative-created issues have a tendency to drive the God/Goddess within each of us further apart, making the rift even greater. When I speak of the God/Goddess within, I am referring to the Yin and Yang—the masculine and feminine energies residing in all of us. The separation within these two is one of the main causes for the imbalance that we are witnessing in our lives and on Planet Earth today.

Of course, all of this is an Ego trip creating the "I'm right and they are wrong" syndrome—a never-ending merry-go-round ride ending up where it started. This will eventually lead us back to the Core Issue to view, when we are willing. When we do become willing to take responsibility, we then see it for what it is—a part of the Illusion's trap.

Yes, all the world is a stage, and we are the actors. However, most of us aren't aware of just why we have chosen the parts we choose. The play does get to be a bit too hot to handle by oneself at times, and both Jim and I knew that we needed each other's assistance in order to rise above the Mass Consciousness Illusion.

Jim arrived as per schedule late Saturday afternoon, and the mission we had agreed to accomplish was about to begin. We both were determined to confront the issues, head-on, for we felt that Spirit had a specific purpose in mind, and that we both were committed to seeing it through.

Since both Jim and I are powerful Masters of The Awakenings guided by Spirit, we knew that this was going to be three very powerful and rewarding days. We were about to put ourselves on the cross of Truth and see Its reflection in Its true Light, not Illusion's false doctrine of pain, suffering and hell's damnation.

This was to be the death of our negative judgments, and the resurrection into the Light of Love, Understanding and Compassion— not only for us, but it would also assist all of Mother Earth's children. The "whole enchilada" did prove to be all we had hoped for, and more.

Sunday morning, around 10 a.m., we could feel the energies of the Masters/Angels starting to build, and we knew that it was time to begin the first session. Jim opted to have his Awakening first.

During the counseling we went to the Core Issue, which was still holding judgments in place, deterring him from accomplishing his "heart's desire" of being accepted by himself and others as the Master that he is. A fragmented part of him was still stuck back in that long ago time, thus robbing him of some of his God-given power.

Upon returning to that time and recognizing how it was affecting his life today, we then went to the Awakening Table. Calling in his Higher Self, and with the assistance of the Masters and Angels of Light, the Awakening began.

I felt the power of The Light assisting me as I stepped into his Energy Field. As the negative energies rose up and were released, I could feel the heavy cloud of negative judgment that had encased him leave, and replaced with Love.

Then the heaviness lifted, and I could feel myself smiling. When the smile turned into a big grin, I knew the Awakening was complete. This is always Spirit's signal to me that it is time to close. I also knew from the messages received that Jim had received what he had asked for—the chains of the past had been severed.

Jim honored his Awakening the rest of Sunday and Monday, allowing the energies to continue working with him. He knew that this had been a big Awakening for him, and wanted to integrate it before he gave me my session.

Tuesday rolled around, and it was my turn. Believe me, I was really ready for one. It had been several months since I had been on the Awakening table—I was always giving an Awakening, not receiving one, for there are no Masters of The Awakenings close by.

Sitting at the table across from Jim, I could feel I was about to reveal to him that which I had never spoken of to anyone regarding the past life, which we both had walked. It had, due to our judgments, left a very painful and indelible mark on our lives. The anger, the guilt, the self blame and judgments of abandonment came pouring out of my mouth—old feelings that had kept me locked up inside of myself for so long. And, of course, tears of regret and release were part of the package. It was time for the healing energies of The Awakening to begin.

I went to the Awakening table, and once again I could feel those loving energies of The Great Masters—Lord Jesus, Mother Mary, The Council of Twelve, Archangel Michael and His Golden Eagles of Light and many more. The room was filled to the brim with beautiful, loving energy.

As the music played, Jim said the prayer, and we were on our way to fulfilling our mission. The first thing I was shown was the deep chasm that separated the masculine and feminine parts of not only myself, but of all of Mother Earth's children. I knew that this was true. That although I had brought my own god/goddess energy together more than once, there still seemed to be a rift between them, which apparently was a reflection of what was being experienced all over the planet. This separation within all of us was creating dis-ease within the total Mass Consciousness on Planet Earth.

I then became aware of Lord Jesus. He was standing on the left side of the table, and Mother Mary was standing on the right. They were holding their hands directly over my head, their fingers touching. I could feel their powerful energy running into my head and down my entire body. It was a beautiful, loving, healing energy. I also saw the chasm that separated the god/goddess within begin to heal—to come together.

I knew that They were not only sending that healing energy of love to me, but that I was being used as the instrument to heal the deep rift between all of humanity. This continued for sometime. Then I became aware that Lord Jesus and Mother Mary had entered into my body, and were nurturing both the masculine and feminine energies of all of Planet Earth's children.

The next thing I knew was that Jim had completed his part in the Awakening and had left the room, as had all of those powerful Beings of Light. I laid there in awe of what I had experienced.

Finally, I knew I should go in and talk to Jim. He was packing, getting ready to go back to his home and little family. Not much was said, for we both knew that we had completed the mission, and that

Spirit was very happy with the results. We hugged and thanked each other and Spirit for assisting us in being of service to the Light, and Jim drove off.

It took me several days to completely return to Planet Earth for I was still processing and working with the energies. Jim said it was the same for him.

It was less than a week later when I began to see why there has been so many with some kind of heart problems. I was experiencing some discomfort in my own heart, and asked myself why wasn't that healed? I knew that, although the actual Awakening had ended, there was still work to be done.

The Awakenings carry that name for that is exactly what they do. They awaken us to the understanding of our commitment to ourselves, and to the unfoldment of the Divine Plan.

I recall one Awakening that I had done on a lady, who was feeling very depressed. She had just moved to a new town, and was having a difficult time in getting her Real Estate business going. Her bills were piling up, and she was in a quandary as to how she was going to meet her obligations.

She came to me for an Awakening, and left feeling much more optimistic. I saw her a couple of days later. Upon asking how she was doing, her reply was "well, I still have those darn bills, but they don't bother me anymore." And I knew that she meant it for she was smiling. Her energy had changed, drastically. Her business took off shortly after that, and now she is on top of her game.

When we raise ourselves out of the lower vibrations of judgment and fear, our outlook on life does change. When this happens, we then create a happier and more abundant life for ourselves. We also will attract others of high vibration to us.

Although I was feeling a very high vibration of love after my Awakening, once again I was seeing Mother with her broken heart. I was also seeing others whom I have felt responsible for in co-creating their own scenarios of heartbreak. My physical heart again was causing me some problems, telling me to go back to those scenarios and fix them.

My knowingness also told me that somewhere there was a missing part of the truth, which needed to be brought to Light. Otherwise, my heart would never completely heal. When we feel we have healed the wounds of the past, and they still rise up to haunt us, then there is usually a missing piece of the truth needing to be looked at. It's sort of like a picture puzzle with some of the pieces missing—the picture cannot be complete until we find those missing pieces.

The words *The Broken Heart Syndrome* kept flashing before my eyes. "What does that mean?" I asked. That is when I began seeing how a "broken heart" can create a physical heart problem, unless the judgment is removed. The Emotional Body gets over-loaded, and then throws the pain off onto the Physical, creating illness and dis-ease.

I called in Spirit of Enlightenment and McAmba to assist me in locating the part of truth that was still missing. I knew that it had to do with forgiveness and responsibility, and that I was going to need some powerful assistance.

So placing myself on the trail of "broken hearts" of past scenarios, which I somehow felt responsible for, I began retracing my steps. However, this time I was viewing them from a higher view point than I had ever seen them before, enabling me to look at those scenarios through the eyes of love without judgment.

This is when I saw the total truth of those scenarios and how I had become ensnared within the trap of the *Broken Heart Syndrome*. I went to my last scenario of that kind, which was with Mother. I had released the anger, the pain, and had felt her forgiveness and love for me.

However, I had not forgiven myself for co-creating that scenario with her, and I had also taken on *full responsibility* for having created that heart-breaking scenario. Thus I was "the bad guy" and needed to be punished. This was why I couldn't seem to forget nor forgive myself—my guilt feelings kept coming up for me to face, which, of course, caused the pain in my heart.

It never dawned on me, until I went back to that last time, that each of us are responsible for our part, *and only our part*, in any scenario we co-create. In other words, Mother had placed herself in that co-creation for her lessons, as had I by placing myself in them for mine. In doing so she, and she alone, was responsible for her part in its creation.

I also saw that by taking on the total responsibility of not only my own part in the scenario, but also hers, I was seeing her as a victim. This then was also making me a victim, as well. Oh yes, judgments are very powerful for they are the creators of karma.

I then began reflecting on my past co-creations of breaking other people's hearts and they breaking mine, in this and other lifetimes. Removing all judgment regarding either side, and knowing that we are all powerful Masters of our own creations, I placed the responsibility where it belonged—squarely on the shoulders of each of us. In doing so, no longer am I carrying the double load of being responsible for others as well as myself. As I have said before, we are here to experience and learn, and I thank all who assisted me in the co-creations. This feels so right on, and has lightened my load considerably for I have learned to love without judgment.

Looking back over other lifetimes, as well as this one, I could see how we have been controlled by our negative emotions. They really can do a number on us until we understand and release them, especially our fears.

Some, who understand the power of fear, will use it as a weapon to control the masses. Religions have done it, as have our governments. Why do you think the words "Weapons of Mass Destruction" have been repeated, over and over again. They paint a picture of horror and death, sending us plunging out of our inner balance. We then do insane acts in order to protect ourselves.

We each carry our own arsenal of "Weapons of Self Destruction," which, if not handled, will rise up and destroy us. The most powerful one is fear, from which all other negative emotions stem. Then there is jealousy, hatred, blame, greed, anger. I'm certain that each of you have bumped up against each of these and, of course, there are many more.

By the way, I have found that anger can be a two-edged sword. If recognized and exploded, it will lift you into a higher vibration. However, if shoved down, ignored, and allowed to fester, it will end up creating depression. Then when it does explode, and it will at sometime or other, it will tear ones life apart along with those it is vented at.

So what has our own individual Weapons of Self-Destruction got to do with Weapons of Mass Destruction? Everything! Think of the thousands of people acting out their fears of being controlled, or of being killed by those who are feeling the same way about them. Thus we give our power away, as we band together in our fear and anger at the thought of having our freedom taken from us.

We build weapons of mass destruction in order to protect ourselves, while those we fear do the same thing. Once fear takes over, our sanity along with our freedom goes out the window. No one can be truly free and fear. Fear becomes our captor and we its prisoner. In other words, we each should take responsibility for self, and handle our own inner Weapons of Self-Destruction. If we did, then we no longer would create the need for negative games of war and retaliation.

Those words *Let there be peace on Earth and let it begin with me* holds the truth to the salvation of not only ourselves, but for all residing on our beautiful Mother Earth. Unless we do, I'm certain that more and more weapons of mass destruction will be created from our fears.

Yes, my path has been one of experiencing and learning, sharing and co-creating, judging and letting go. We are constantly reflecting to others what we need to experience to enhance our awareness, and others are doing the same to us. Then we co-create scenarios which we judge, and when the timing is right will realize that it was all a matter of choice. Thus we become more discerning as to what we choose to experience.

Isn't it amazing the games we choose to play?

We areSpirit
in physical form

Created
within the loving
Essence
of

THE GREAT I AM

ENLIGHTENED

Being Enlightened is our natural state
All else is Illusion

My journey, this lifetime, has taken me from irresponsibility and unawareness into high awareness and total responsibility. However, I do have to admit that the beginning poem portrayed my life very accurately. It has been, most definitely, a roller-coaster ride, as well as a jumbled picture puzzle.

Would I have exchanged any of it for a less traumatic path? Evidently not, for I now have come to realize fully what Jimmy meant when he said over and over again, *Take the judgment off—it's perfect just the way it is.*

Nor would I go back and repeat the same scenarios again—why should I? I have gleaned from those experiences the knowledge, the love, and the understanding for which so many lifetimes I have searched. I now realize that they have always been with me. Thus I no longer go back into my habitual ritual of creating scenarios of trauma, fear, and pain with my judgments.

I also have the ability to separate the wheat from the chaff, along with the awareness to know the difference. Until I achieved this, I was unable to be discerning in what I chose to experience. I now am completely satisfied with what I have accomplished.

This happened when my arrogant Gold Ray was merged with the more loving and compassionate Silver Ray while receiving an awakening. It was a wonderful experience, balancing my ego along with my inner god/goddess/child.

Just prior to that Awakening I had received this message entitled THE GOLD AND SILVER RAYS from Lord Jesus:

Within your very center lies the Gold Ray. It is located within the solar plexus Chakra, running upward and downward throughout the physical body. It may, because of negativity, become blocked. This may set up a push-pull effect within you, creating confusion.

The Gold Ray is who you are—your essence. It is a vibration, powerful and, when out of control, can be very arrogant and destructive—like a great wind that sweeps away everything in its path, destroying yourself as well.

When tempered with Unconditional Love, It then is within Its balance and can create wondrous things of beauty, enhancing the Light.

The Silver Ray is also very powerful. However, It does not carry the arrogance and independent stubbornness of the Gold Ray. It is more tolerant and integrated, thus less destructive unto Itself and others. The Gold Ray has come to Earth for a lesson in tolerance, love and balance. The Silver Ray is here to assist the Gold Ray in becoming balanced.

The Gold Ray is of The Eagles—such as Archangel Michael. They are The Warriors for The Light.

The Silver Ray is of the Loving, Gentle and Compassionate Essence— The Christed Energy of Unconditional Love.

When the Gold and Silver Rays integrate and become as one—i.e. running simultaneously, yet distinct within their own properties—you then have the true power of The Warrior and The Teacher/Healer wielding the Sword of Love.

There are other Rays. However, the Gold Ray was the first creation of The Great I AM, thus it is within each and every one. However, because of its arrogance and non-compassion, it soon became apparent that a softer, more tolerant Ray needed to be created to balance and offset the Gold Ray's powerful impact. This has not been an easy task due to the stubborn arrogance of The Gold Ray.

New energies are arriving on the Planet, thus the task is becoming less difficult as balance takes place. The Gold Ray is being tempered with Unconditional Love. The Silver Ray is also coming into Its own balance, becoming the mighty warrior using Unconditional Love as Its sword.

As the two Rays merge more and more into each other's energy, you then will rise to the highest vibration of all—into the Love and Light of The All That Is—working as one for the highest good of Planet Earth and The Divine Plan. With the coming together of these two awesome energies, a higher level of awareness and love has been obtained, opening up the portals of Fifth Dimension so all may enter.

The Fifth Dimension is no longer an unobtainable dream, but is becoming reality. The Kingdom of God is at hand for those who have allowed their Gold Ray to be washed in the waters of Unconditional Love.

All is in perfect Divine Order.

I AM YOUR TEACHER—YOUR HEALER. I AM LORD JESUS THE CHRIST

How does it feel to be Enlightened? The best way for me to describe it, from my point of view, is to repeat some of those wonderful words to the song "On A Clear Day". They go something like this: *On a clear day, rise and look around you, and you'll know who you are. Then nothing can astound you, for the glow of your Being outshines any star. You'll be part of every mountain, sea and shore. You will hear both far and near the words you have been searching for. Then on that Clear Day you will see forever and ever more.*

Upon rising above the murky clouds of the Illusion, I began seeing clearly all of those pitfalls that I had blindly blundered into on my path. It was like walking out of a very heavy dense fog into a beautiful bright, clear day, with nothing clouding my vision. I saw clearly, for the first time, that I was a part of everything. This gave me a much more expanded view of our connection to all life.

I know that there is war, pain, suffering, fear, and anger exploding all over the Planet. However, they have little, if any, affect upon me. Once attaining a higher point of view, I can now look upon other people's creations as their path that they have chosen to walk. Thus there is no judgment on my part. This then frees me to observe without becoming emotionally involved.

I have learned not to be judgmental of any scenario, or those creating it. If I did then I would become a part of their scenarios, which would plunge me back down into the fray again. Having walked in that dark cloud of unkowingness and unawareness for so many lifetimes, this joyous feeling of having all my fragmented parts united is indescribable.

I am now aware that in order to have a sane and happy life, I must always walk in integrity and unconditional love. In order to do this, I also must take on my own responsibility—for self only.

In order to maintain my own sanity, as I walk within this insanity that is being created here on Mother Earth, I have set up some specific guidelines for me to follow. They act as a reminder to me of my responsibilities, and to whom I am responsible for. This keeps me from stumbling over myself, causing me to fall back down into the old ways of Illusion's habitual-ritual judgments. Here is the list that I adhere to:

There is only one person I am responsible for, and that person is me. Thus I will take the responsibility to accept into my life only that which is for my highest good, and which will make me happy.

When co-creating a scenario, I will remember to allow everyone to take on their own responsibility in the co-creation, and not burden myself with all of their extra baggage. I know that each of us has lessons to learn, and must walk their individual path the way they choose to walk it—not how another thinks they should. When allowed to do so, without judgment or interference from someone else, then they too will learn what they need for their highest good and evolvement. (This is especially true for parents, for our dreams and expectations get all tangled up with our children's. Thus we believe that we KNOW what is best for them. We need to love them, unconditionally, and let them grow.)

I will always walk in my integrity, with no judgment of how others walk their path. However, I will also be very observant, using discernment as to whether or not I wish to join them in co-creating a scenario—it just might be that their scenario is not for me.

I will look upon every scenario that I put myself into as a learning experience. I then will be able to Get the lesson and move on. This way I do not stick myself in judgment,. Thus I let go, loving it for the lesson, and always remembering to thank those who co-created the scenario with me.

I will stay out of judgment, which will also keep me out of the past. Thus I will be able to live a much happier, more productive life. I know that when I try to create from past negative scenarios, the results will be less than optimum. Thus it is highly important that I always stay in the present moment of now. The past is gone. Only the judgment I place upon it keeps me shackled to it.

I will always remember that: *"YOU CANNOT LOVE AND JUDGE AT THE SAME TIME—FOR IT IS IMPOSSIBLE."*

I will always be gentle and kind to myself, loving myself and others unconditionally. In doing so, I then will always create that which is for my highest good, without blame or shame. Thus I will avoid the pitfalls of illness, pain and traumatic experiences.

I know that I am a Master, creating my life for my own, as well as for other's, highest good. In realizing this, I will honor the Master that I am, making the commitment to no longer play the game of being a victim. In other words, I am taking responsibility for self. This is when the rest will fall into Divine Order.

And I will always remember that Judgment will trap me, and Love will free me. And that Until I love myself, unconditionally, I can not truly love.

All of this has to do with being responsible to and for one's self, allowing everyone else to shoulder their own responsibilities. In doing so we will find peace and joy as we walk in the Love of The Great I AM, for we are Its glorious reflection.

This does not mean that I will not assist others on our path to the Light. Far from it, for I know that we are all connected, thus what affects another will also affect me.

I will always look with understanding, compassion and empathy upon my fellow man's chosen path. Thus I am more than willing to assist anyone who is willing to take on their own responsibility for the scenario they have chosen to either co-create or create by themselves.

In making my decisions of should I or shouldn't I, I sometimes call upon that beautiful and very wise prayer, which I learned during my stint in AA. This was back in my earlier fogged-up days. It is short, and sweet and to the point. Its wisdom always assists me in making decisions as to whether or not to become involved in someone else's creations.

I'm certain you have heard it at one time or another, but it is worthy of repeating, so here goes: *God grant me the serenity to accept the things I cannot change, the courage to change the thing I can, and the wisdom to know the difference.*

Using this assists me in keeping myself out of the booby-trap of sticking my nose into what other people are either creating or co-creating. Thus I have become very aware that if it isn't for my highest good, then to become involved will not be for theirs either. Experience and lessons are still the name of this game we call life.

Yes, I have walked many paths, and have experienced many scenarios on my path out of darkness into the Light. However, no longer am I forever searching for that illusive butterfly of peace and love. That part of me, which I watched leave when I was a child, has now returned, and has integrated within my heart, setting me free.

It didn't happen all at once but gradually. As a small seed of understanding myself grew, so did my love for myself and everyone else. This, in turn, began the process of transforming my fears, doubts and judgments into blossoms of love—the most powerful vibration of all.

Inch by inch, step by step, painful as it appeared at the time, I did evolve. I now have this wonderful feeling of freedom—of self-realization and knowingness, which, in turn, has erased all question of why I chose this path to walk.

I no longer ask, "Who am I?" I know beyond a shadow of a doubt that I am a loving Being, experiencing and evolving, created by the Great Mother/Father God within the love of The All That Is.

I am Infinity in physical form on Planet Earth. I also know that there is no death, only life as Spirit experiences Itself in various forms of transformation. God has spread before each of us a banquet to partake of in whatever way we each chooses. Choose wisely, my friend. Live each moment to the fullest, and love whatever scenario you choose to experience.

For Love is and always will be the highest and most powerful vibration that you can achieve. *It is God's gift to all of us.*

ALLOW
with no resistance

LOVE
without judgment

EVERYTHING

When you do, you will know true
freedom

VOICES IN THE WIND

I hear voices in the wind
They're saying that a change is coming in
But oh, my friend, this isn't the end
For love will see us through
The love I have for you

*L*isten, be willing to hear—to be a part of the whole, not separate
from. The secret to all life is blending, not resisting—loving, not judging.

Once again, I was being given a valuable message. Sitting with my
back against a big brother pine, my fanny was planted firmly on a rock.
A sparkling blue lake spread out before me as white fluffy clouds floated
in a sky as blue as the lake.

Everything was so very quiet, except for the wind as it softly played
with the golden aspen leaves, sending messages for all who would hear.

For me, this beautiful mountain known as Grand Mesa has become
a cathedral where I can go and commune with God in the way I have

come to know Him/Her. No man-made cathedral ever has, or ever could be as sacred—at least not to me.

I hear beautiful music, fully orchestrated, all around. There is no yesterday, no tomorrow, as I blend with the water, the sky, the rocks and trees. The song of birds enhances the magic of the moment.

Be still and know that I am God! These words, spoken so many times in churches, have taken on a more expanded meaning. No longer are they just words, for I know in my heart that this power we call God is truly THE GREAT I AM, which I am a part of.

Nor do I find myself running helter-skelter, looking for that elusive butterfly of peace and love. It has finally made itself known to me— patiently waiting deep in my heart to be recognized, where it has been all along.

I am aware that there still is fear, greed and judgment on Planet Earth, exploding into war, poverty, hate and disease. All this mankind has created as they explore the negative polarity for their own evolution.

However, I choose not to get caught up in that which I know is not of my vibration. The excitement of the chase no longer excites me— for me there is nothing to chase after, so why should it?

I have gleaned much from my stay on Planet Earth. I came here, lifetimes ago, as a Gold Ray, full of ego and disdain, pumped up in my haughty and judgmental attitude, with neither understanding nor compassion.

From that lofty perch, I was reduced in stature and power, so that I was forced to look at the other side of the coin—the negative side. My high-and-mighty attitude was diminished to what one might liken to a caterpillar, crawling inch by inch toward enlightenment.

The metamorphosis of myself was, at times, excruciatingly traumatic and slow. I found myself walking in the lower vibrations, thus being controlled by the demanding voice of Fear with all of its negative sidekicks. In other words, no longer was I in the driver's seat.

Some time ago I was given the whole picture of how this came about. I found myself feeling somewhat put upon and angry, instead of grateful, and I was beginning to view my many experiences as struggle instead of appreciating the awareness I had gleaned from those many lifetimes. So I started asking "why me"?

This must have opened up the records, for I found myself talking to MeAmba, my Higher Self. I was being shown a time before making my appearance on Planet Earth. The conversation went something like this:

I was saying, "Let me experience it all. I can handle anything that Planet Earth can throw at me." I was either being told or had volunteered to come here. In either case, I had some lessons to learn regarding my arrogant attitude, and to have my Gold Ray blended with the more compassionate Silver Ray.

"So Be It," was the reply. Thus my stay on Planet Earth became a long, drawn-out play as I was handed different parts to act out in many different lifetimes.

It wasn't until quite recently, while receiving an Awakening, that I felt my Gold Ray being washed clean by the Silver Ray. It was, for me, not unlike the baptisms that Jesus performed while incarnated here. It was the total surrender of one's ego—denouncing the path chosen by the arrogant and non-compassionate Gold Ray, and embracing the loving, compassionate path of the Silver Ray. The blending of those two powerful Rays can be awesome.

Like the caterpillar, I, for so long, slowly inched my way toward my enlightenment, lifetime after lifetime—sometimes slipping, falling back into old ways, going down blind alleys—always looking for that perfect me, wrapped in my cocoon of negativity.

Then one day I wake up. No longer am I wrapped in my cocoon of forgetfulness but sitting on a rock, leaning against a big brother tree just Being. I hear the wind gently moving through the trees, whispering:

The music of life is all around you.
Be still and listen with your heart.
Feel God's loving arms around you,
For love is the essence where all life must start.

The beauty of life is all around you.
Open your eyes and you will see.
The illusion's gone, only joy surrounds you.
You've found your wings now fly, for you are free!

YOUR INNER BALANCE IS
THE KEY TO LOVE

AND

LOVE IS THE KEY TO ALL LIFE

BUTTERFLY

transformation and new beginnings

A butterfly never asks why. it only allows
with love the beauty of its unfoldment
Be the butterfly and enjoy your journey
       wherever it may lead you

It is not the finished product that brings you joy
It is the step by step of creating in each and every moment
Let go of the past—forget the future.
Love yourself unconditionally.
All of whom and what you are
The part of you that creates
The part of you that is being created.

Love transforms the meanest of tasks into joy.
Beauty is in the eyes of the beholder.
Beauty is the laughter and the joy of the child

Your life is yours to create
Create whatever brings you joy—happiness

Look upon everything through the eyes of love
And watch the dark clouds of the illusion
The ugliness—the pain—the fear
       Vanish in the warmth of your smile

I wish you a joyful journey on your path to enlightenment

BVG